THE **ONE THING** THAT **CHANGED EVERYTHING**

To

From

I wish for you a life of wealth, health, and happiness; a life in which you give to yourself the gift of patience, the virtue of reason, the value of knowledge, and the influence of faith in your own ability to dream about and to achieve worthy rewards.

– Jim Rohn

Published by
Lessons From Network
www.LessonsFromNetwork.com

Distributed by
Lessons From Network
P.O. Box 93927
Southlake, TX 76092
817-379-2300
www.LessonsFromNetwork.com/books

ISBN-13: 978-0-9983125-5-2 (Paperback)

Printed in the United States of America.

THE **ONE THING** THAT **CHANGED EVERYTHING**

**Receive Your Special Bonuses for
Buying *The One Thing That Changed Everything* Book**

To Receive Your Special Bonuses
Send an Email to gifts@LessonsFromOneThingBook.com

DISCLAIMER

The information in this book is not meant to replace the advice of a certified professional. Please consult a licensed advisor in matters relating to your livelihood including your mental and physical health, finances, business, legal matters, family planning, education, and spiritual practices.

If you choose to attempt any of the methods mentioned in this book, the authors and publisher advise you to take full responsibility for your safety and know your limits. The authors and publisher are not liable for any damages or negative consequences from any treatment, action, application, or preparation to any person reading or following the information in this book.

Neither the publisher nor the individual authors shall be liable for any physical, psychological, emotional, financial, or commercial damages, including, but not limited to, special, incidental, consequential, or other damages to the readers of this book.

The content of each chapter is the sole expression and opinion of its authors and not necessarily that of the publisher. No warranties or guarantees are expressed or implied by the publisher's choice to include any of the content in this volume.

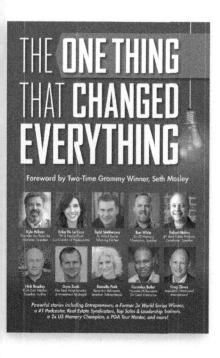

To order additional copies, including quantity discounts, of *The One Thing That Changed Everythings* see below.

SPECIAL QUANTITY PRICING:
(Retail $17.97)

1	$11.97 ea
2-9	$8.97 ea
10-24	$5.97 ea
25-99	$4.47 ea
100+	$2.97 ea

Plus shipping. Based on location and weight.

TO ORDER PLEASE:

1. *Order online
   www.LessonsFromNetwork.com/Books
2. Call 817-379-2300
2. E-Mail: info@lessonsfromnetwork.com
4. Via mail: **Lessons From Network**
   P.O. Box 93927
   Southlake, TX 76092

You can mix and match these additional titles:

- *Life-Defining Moments from Bold Thought Leaders*
- *Passionistas: Tips, Tales and Tweetables From Women Pursuing Their Dreams*
- *The Little Black Book of Fitness: Breakthrough Insights from Mind, Body & Soul Warriors*
- *Mom & Dadpreneurs: Stories, Strategies, and Tips from Super Achievers in Family and Business*

*Order online at www.LessonsFromNetwork.com/Books and receive additional bonuses from Kyle Wilson and other thought leaders!

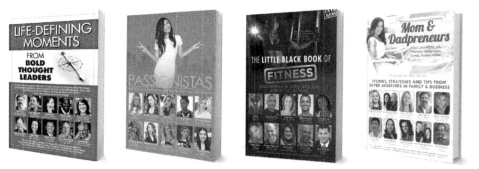

Order online www.LessonsFromNetwork.com/Books

Dedication

To Mom, Dad, Jim Rohn and other angels looking down who inspire and light my path.

Acknowledgement

To Takara Sights for your endless hours of work and passion in this book as our editor and project manager! This makes book number five for you and me! A thousand praises! You are a rockstar! #millennialsrule

Foreword

by Seth Mosley

I met Kyle Wilson through Robert Helms, who is also part of this book. We were backstage at an event and got to connect over one of our shared passions—music. Kyle overheard me sharing a story about working with bands and felt led to share with me that Switchfoot was his favorite band. Funny enough, I had just had Switchfoot's frontman Jon Foreman over to my studio the week before to produce a single. Needless to say, we instantly connected over this little detail, and have had an incredible relationship since then.

What I appreciate about Kyle is that he understands that being successful is all about surrounding yourself with quality people. And the common thread that quality people share is great philosophy—namely, that they all want to truly make a difference in the lives of others. That is why I am honored to be a part of this book. It is full of people who are movers and shakers, people who found their "one thing" in life and are using it to impact culture.

I had my "one thing moment" when I was a touring musician. I had a band that was on the road full-time, doing about 300 dates a year. I was trying to build my empire, and it wasn't working. I guess you could say that it was my favorite failure. Why? Because in that failure I learned to be a servant. For me, much more important than me being the guy at the front of the stage is helping others who have that dream get there. There's a saying that "If you lift people up, they tend to take you with them." That realization launched me into an incredibly successful role behind the scenes as a songwriter and Grammy-winning producer, which in turn, has given me the platform to mentor up-and-coming musicians on their journeys. My one thing was learning to be a servant. The irony is that serving was what led me to success.

Kyle is a master of teaching people how to champion others—how to tell others' stories. This incredibly servant-minded mission is another reason why I am drawn to people just like him, and all the other mission-minded folks in this book. If you learn nothing else from Kyle Wilson, learn this. Many people spend careers thinking they have to be the person at the front of the stage. He has learned that serving others in their callings is just as important, and he has helped me learn to master that role in our Full Circle Music Academy and the other ventures I am now a part of. He helped us build our academy from 0 to $100,000 in Year 1. And it is continually growing with the ideas and philosophies I've gotten from him.

More than anything, I'm honored to be a part of this book because its philosophy will literally change peoples' lives. We will see people overcome challenges in health, overcome challenges in business, overcome challenges in relationships, and in many other areas. I'm sure of it. I know many of these writers and their families personally and know they are the real deal.

Like anything, a book is only as good as what you do with it. So take these philosophies and put them into practice, even if it just for the next month! I guarantee you'll see massive shifts in your life and success. You might even find your one thing that will change everything while you read.

Kyle, thanks for having me be a part. Reader, I hope I get to see you on the cover of one of Kyle's books soon. :)

Seth Mosley

2x Grammy Winner, Billboard #1 Music Producer of the Year, Song Writer of the Year, Founder of Full Circle Music

TABLE OF CONTENTS

"Don't wish it was easier; wish you were better. Don't wish for less problems; wish for more skills. Don't wish for less challenges; wish for more wisdom."

– Jim Rohn

CHAPTER 1

The Greatest Lesson From My Mentor, Friend and 18 Year Biz Partner, Jim Rohn

by Kyle Wilson

In my early days as a newbie seminar promoter (four years before I launched Jim Rohn International in 1993), I was promoting a small event in Dallas. I had booked Jim Rohn for a day long seminar starting at 10am and going till 4pm.

Typically, I would arrive around 6:30am to make sure the stage, room, and tables were all set up correctly, and then my team and I would set up product tables and get everything ready for when attendees arrived. Often, people would start to show up as early as 1-2 hours before the start time.

Well, for this seminar, I was in for a bit of a shock. I arrived at the meeting room early, only to find it packed full of people! Another event was already going on in MY meeting room! What!?

I instantly went into panic mode. When I found the hotel staff, they assured me everything was okay since that meeting would end by 9:30 and they could do a quick turnaround by 10.

Well that's NOT how it works. It takes hours to set up the room, stage, sound, and product tables, plus we would have attendees showing up early to get the best seats before the current meeting was even going to be over.

I went into solution mode and asked if they could give us another room. Answer: No—they were booked solid (one of the reasons they tried to sneak this other event in).

Now I'm beyond upset and panicked. My first thoughts were all the expectations of those who had purchased tickets and their busy schedules. And I have to admit, I then started thinking about all the refunds that were going to happen as a result.

Then it escalated. I was worrying about how all this would reflect upon me in the eyes of not only the attendees but also in my esteem with the man I had booked to speak, my future mentor and business partner, Jim Rohn.

All attempts to find a solution had been exhausted. Now I faced how to best communicate this to the folks showing up and to Jim.

Around 8am, Jim came strolling down to check in before going to have a bit of breakfast. I braced myself to share the really bad news.

I humbly and sheepishly told him I had somehow dropped the ball and allowed the hotel to overlap us with another event. I explained that at the very best we would be able to start at 11 and that we would need to explain what was going on with attendees and ask them to wait.

I'll never forget this next moment for the rest of my life. After sharing the bad news and making it clear we were out of options, Jim just calmly looked at me and said,

"Kyle it will be okay. It's not like a good friend died. Now, that would be a problem"

"We will just have to explain to everyone the circumstances. They will understand and will wait. And I will make it up to them by going longer and I will make this my all-time, best seminar."

WOW!

What a paradigm shift! And what an incredible life lesson for me to learn from my future mentor. "It's not like a good friend just died!"

That's perspective!

Since, I have used that line and the real meaning behind it to gain perspective when things don't go the way I intended.

Now what made this wisdom even more special was that I had never heard Jim say those words privately or on stage ever (and would never hear him say them after). I went on to be Jim's 18 year business partner. I was executive producer on every audio and video series. I published every book and put on every event from 1993 to 2007. So, I knew him and his work. It was just the perfect word, in season, from one of the greatest men I've ever known.

I will always be grateful for all the remarkable lessons and wisdom Jim passed on to me beginning with the first time I promoted him in 1990, through starting Jim Rohn International in 1993, and up until his passing in 2009.

Jim, one more time, thank you for your friendship and mentorship in my life. I will forever be honored and blessed! I promise to always share your message and the impact it has had on me and so many others.

With love,
Kyle

TWEETABLE

It's not like a good friend died. Now, that would be a problem. Always keep things in perspective.

Kyle Wilson, Founder of Jim Rohn International, YourSuccessStore, LessonsFromNetwork.com and KyleWilson.com. Kyle has filled big event rooms and produced 100s of programs including titles by Jim Rohn, Brian Tracy, Zig Ziglar, Denis Waitley, and recently the books Life-Defining Moments, Passionistas, The Little Black Book of Fitness, *and* Mom & Dadpreneurs. *Kyle leads the Kyle Wilson Inner Circle Mastermind and The Kyle Wilson Mentoring Group. He is the author of* 52 Lessons I Learned *from* Jim Rohn and Other Great Legends I Promoted *and co-author of* Chicken Soup For the Entrepreneur's Soul! *Go to KyleWilson.com/connect to download Free books and audio and to connect on social media.*

CHAPTER 2

The Power of Giving and How It Transformed My Life!

by Bruce Aleo

First, I would like to thank God for all the gifts, lessons, and blessings he's provided for me throughout my life, because I do know one thing for sure, without God nothing is possible.

Growing up with ADHD and a serious case of hyperactivity, my identical twin brother and I were quite a handful in school and out. Paying attention in school was very difficult unless it was for one of my three favorite subjects, that's right, only three: gym, math, and art. Art class was my favorite of the three because I had so much passion for drawing. It was the one thing that always captured my attention and kept me focused. I remember times in other classes, especially the ones that didn't interest me, where I would stare out the window, watch the leaves blowing on the trees and say to myself, someday I want to work out there with nature, fresh air, green grass, and beautiful, colorful plants. That's where I belong, not in this classroom.

When I was 16 years old, I was still in the 8th grade. That's right, you read correctly. I was still in the 8th grade when I should've been graduating from high school, and that's not the bad news. I was just told by my principal and submaster that I was failing in most of my subjects and that they were keeping me back for another year in the 8th grade. Feeling unhappy and very disappointed, I knew school wasn't for me. I went to my mother and told her that I wanted to quit school because I didn't want to waste another five years of my life. If I stayed in school, I would be 21 years old and graduating high school at the same time all my friends were graduating college.

She asked me if I had any plans or goals for what I wanted to do if I quit school, and I told her that I wanted to start my own landscaping business because I felt that landscaping would allow me to use my creativity where I always wanted to be, outdoors.

She looked me right in the eyes and said, "Whatever you put your mind to in life, I know you will achieve it." She believed in me, and that was exactly what I needed to hear.

So, the very next day I went to my school and told my teachers, principal, and submaster what I planned to do. I remember it like it was yesterday. My submaster reacted with the most negativity. He actually laughed and said that I was making a very poor decision. He said that if I quit school, I would never amount to anything. I would never go anywhere, and no one would ever hire me without a high school diploma. And that is when I felt that fire burning, you know the one, when someone tells you that you can't do something that you already believe you can. The more he said I would fail, the more confident I felt that I would succeed. So I just said, "We'll see."

So the very next day after quitting school I was out and about, knocking on doors and asking homeowners if they needed any landscaping such as lawn mowing, hedge trimming, or just general yard clean-ups as I had done at my grandmother's house and for other people in the neighborhood since I was 14 years old.

Only having a pocket full of determination, I scraped up the little money I had to buy educational landscaping books, books on how to start a business, marketing books, and the necessary landscaping tools I needed to do basic landscaping for small jobs. I knew that if I didn't learn, I couldn't earn. Even though I knew that I didn't have much money, I never once doubted myself. I was so passionate, and I believed that if I woke up early every morning and went after my goals, it would all be worth it in the end.

Well, about a year later, I remember driving around and looking for homes that needed landscaping. I noticed a beautiful home in Melrose, MA in a very expensive neighborhood. I knew that if I could get this account and landscape this beautiful house, it would lead to many bigger jobs in the area. So I pulled over, walked up to the door, and rang the bell. When the door opened, I introduced myself and told the gentleman I noticed his hedges where overgrown and that I could trim them. He asked me how much I would charge to trim them, and I said, "I want to be honest with you, I've never worked on a house this big before, so I don't know exactly how much to charge." So I said, "I'll tell you what, let me do the work and show you what I can do. Then, just pay me whatever you think I'm worth," not knowing that those were the best words I could have ever said. I spent three long days from morning until night pruning, trimming, and reshaping the hedges and plants and cleaning up everything. I even mowed his lawn which wasn't included in what we talked about. When I was done, he said that no one he had worked with in the past ever took the time as I had to prune off all the dead limbs and shape the hedges like I did. He said that they never looked better. When he handed me the check, I was shocked. The amount was for three times more than what I would've ever asked for. But that wasn't the bonus. The bonus was when he said he wanted to refer me to his sister who lived around the corner on the golf course who also needed landscaping. After building a relationship with him and his sister, they both kept referring me to all their friends. The lesson I learned from this was to always go with your instincts. I had a nothing to lose attitude.

If you never ask, the answer is always no.

I come from a family of givers. My mother raised us alone, so it wasn't easy for her. She had to do double the work and support us alone. She raised us with Biblical principles and taught us that there is no greater gift than the gift of giving. "You never lose when you help someone else. It always comes back to you one way or another."

Many years later, I often found myself thinking about these words of wisdom and how I could apply them to my life and business. In 1995 I was driving along the shore past an island in Saugus, MA and I noticed it was rundown, weed infested, and could definitely use a little TLC. I called town hall and asked to speak to the town manager. When he came on the phone, I introduced myself and told him that I'd like to donate my services to dress up the town property that was being neglected. I would be willing to pay for all the materials if necessary. All I asked in return was that I be allowed to leave two permanent signs at each end of the island so that I could get a little exposure. I told him that it would be a win/win for both of us, and he agreed. He loved the idea and said that I had the go-ahead whenever I was ready. So I was there the very next day.

After completely redesigning the island with new topiary evergreens shrubs, flowering plants, perennial grasses, cobblestone borders, different colored stones, mulch, and a beautiful plum leaf sand cherry tree in the center, I received a call from the town manager thanking me for doing such a wonderful job.

He then asked if I would be interested in taking on another town property in Saugus that was going to be a focus point in coming months, and I said, "Sure." So we made an appointment to meet at the corner of Walnut and Water Street in Saugus, MA. At the time this was just a wooded area with overgrown grass. He explained that the town would be putting up traffic lights there at this three-way intersection and they were installing a big Welcome to Saugus sign at the corner. Let me just say that this property was more than ten times bigger than the small island I just landscaped, so I knew it would cost me a lot more money. Not even hesitating, I said, "I'm in." After three weeks of work and all was said and done, it cost me a little over $50,000 to design that area. $50,000 that I didn't have. Thank God for credit cards!

Everyone, and I mean everyone, called me crazy. They said, "Fifty grand? You could've put that money on a down payment on a house, advertised and took out full page ads, purchased trucks," and so on. All the things they said would've helped me, and only me. I knew that giving back to the community was a good deed, and I felt privileged and blessed to have the opportunity to display my work on public town property for so many people to see and enjoy.

A couple of weeks later, I received a call from the Massachusetts Institute of Technology in Cambridge, MA. They asked me to come out and give them a design for one of their courtyards, so I scheduled an appointment to meet with them. When I arrived, they gave me the grand tour of MIT and told me all about this amazing place of education, how they generate their own electricity, and so much more. It was a learning experience in and of itself. After doing a walkthrough of the courtyard and giving them design ideas of what I could do there, they said they wanted to move forward. I thanked them and then asked them how they heard of my company or who referred me so I could thank them. The project manager told me, "No one referred you. Actually, you just landscaped a town property in Saugus, and I live right next to it. I've been watching you and the beautiful transformation you and your team have done there."

That is when I had my aha moment. I realized that doing the work I love to do and giving back to others at the same time was a perfect recipe for success. Live to give! So I proceeded to apply more and more of this idea to my life and my business. I continued to take on more adopt-a-site programs in multiple towns and even other businesses such as the Saugus, MA and Melrose, MA family YMCAs, Rosie's Place in Boston the first women's homeless shelter in the country www.rosiesplace.org, two MA post office locations, and vocational schools. I started training the students taking agriculture classes as well. The more I gave, the better I felt about myself. I could see that the more I gave, the more people wanted to work with me. People really appreciated how I was beautifying communities. Little by little, I was creating credibility and setting my business apart from the rest by giving.

One day we were landscaping a home in Melrose, MA, and across the street I noticed a car pull into the driveway. When the man stepped out of the car, I recognized him right away. It was my old submaster from junior high school. I called out his name and waved to him, then I walked over to properly say hi. We talked for a while and then he told me that he saw this landscaping company's signs and work all over town. He said, "You chose a great company to work for. They do beautiful work and have a great reputation. That is when I said, "I don't work for this company, I own this company. I started building this company right after quitting school and I've been swinging away at it ever since."

He reached out his hand, looked me right in the eyes and said, "I'm sorry for doubting you, and I'm proud of you and what you've accomplished with your life. You proved me wrong."

I said, "There's no need to apologize. I didn't do this to prove anyone wrong." I did this to prove myself right and for all the people who believed in me, especially my mom. I even named my company Done Right Landscaping considering that with a name like that, I couldn't go wrong.

Today, my business is more successful than ever before and continues to grow each and every year. We've won countless awards and competitions in multiple cities all over Massachusetts. I've been fortunate enough to have been previewed on HGTV and Close-Up TV News. I have created a sustainable business that runs whether or not I am physically there. This flexibility allows me to travel four months out of the year, most of which I spend in amazingly beautiful Thailand and other exotic countries where I'm always learning new designs and getting more creative ideas to share with my customers. It's a pretty awesome life that I thank God for everyday!

"Giving is not just about making a donation, it's about making a difference."
— Kathy Calvin

TWEETABLE
It's not about proving others wrong, it's about proving yourself right.

Bruce Aleo - President & Founder of Done Right Landscape & Construction Co., Inc is a multi-award winning designer as previewed on HGTV and Close-up TV News. He has extensive experience and knowledge in all phases of landscape design, hardscaping, and softscaping. With four locations throughout the Boston area, he has provided residential, commercial and institutional landscaping for over 30 years.

www.DoneRightLandscape.com

CHAPTER 3

Set Yourself Free

by Erika De La Cruz

It had been four years since I had seen my mother. And there I sat, waiting for her to arrive. My thumb brushed the side of my phone as I listened to the drawn-out rings.

"...Hello," replied the shaky voice of my mother. "I'm sorry, I got off the train."

"What do you mean you got off the train, are you here already?"

"...No, I got halfway and then I got scared. I boarded another one back to San Jose."

My mom was now heading the opposite direction from where I stood on my Los Angeles balcony, something that had happened plenty of times before and to which my usual response would have been tears, some form of verbal frustration, or righteousness. But this time was different. I cracked a small smile and said, "Mom, get off at the next stop. Look up every train still heading here and get on one of them."

My mom's voice cracked. "I can't! You don't understand how much I've suffered. Being away from you, being on my own, my family. I know you are going to judge me when I get there! I don't think I'm dressed right either, I don't look good right now!"

A vast array of excuses left her lips. The words painted a picture of what had taken place between us the last six years since she decided to retreat from society and her family into a cloud of confusion for all of us and for her. We were left with the ongoing struggle of trying to identify if she did or did not want help. We were left with the pain of trying to identify if drugs or disillusion was the issue. We had years full of tense departures as each member of the family gave up, and we had, the worse for me, long, painful periods of nothing—no phone number to reach her, no email, no address, just my memories and a resolution that our relationship was over.

This time was different though. The month before, I discovered what could make that difference—forgiveness. Forgiveness whether she sought it or not. And in turn, I asked for hers, whether I thought I had anything to apologize for or not. This was why she was on her way. Because I had made a vow to just love her. I decided to stop putting our relationship in the "SHOULD" box of mother-daughter and instead create it from "someone who loves me who I need to love too." So, in accordance with that decision, I enlisted my partner to look up the train schedule, looped him into our call, and together we created a "no negotiation train ride support team."

My partner's jovial, but stern voice echoed, "Hello Connie, we're very excited that you are coming to visit us. Which new time would you like, the 4pm this evening or the 6am tomorrow morning?"

After a couple hours of exclamations, explanations, and more fear, she arrived at love in that conversation, and within 24 hours, she arrived at Los Angeles Union Station.

Though brief, we spent two days together. Me, re-familiarizing myself with her scent, her touch, even her humor. Her getting to know my life and even a few of the people in it. For the first time, breakdowns and crises reflected only hurt and a desire to be heard. So I listened. I tried my best to stay in love. And when I fell short, I still would not have traded those moments for isolation. I had developed an ability to not only forgive, but also the perspective for the entire situation to seem unimportant in comparison to spending time with her.

I heard once that harboring ill-will is like drinking poison and waiting for the other person to die. I believe that now. For years I believed –but my mom, –but my family situation, –but my circumstances were too complicated to just "bring love to" to "bring forgiveness to." That's not true. And that, single-handedly, has made the difference not only in one of my most important relationships, but also in my daily routine. Imagine the power you create when you are simply "unaffected." Unaffected by the driver who cut you off, the boss who didn't say thank you, or the friend who you believe has thrown an insult. Forgive them. Love them. Retain your commitment to live a peaceful, loving life. That is when you shift the power back into your own hands. That is when you set yourself free.

TWEETABLE
This time was different. I discovered what could make that difference—forgiveness. Forgiveness whether she sought it or not.

Erika De La Cruz, 27, is a Media & TV Host and Personality, Red Carpet Correspondent and Brand Ambassador of Fashion Week San Diego. She works with The CW TV Network, Variety's Night of the Stars and NBC. She is the Lessons From Network Millennials Expert and is the author of the book Passionistas: Tales, Tips and Tweetables From Women Pursuing Their Dreams.

erikadelacruz.com
erika@erikadelacruz.com
Instagram: @_Erikadelacruz

.

CHAPTER 4

How to Sell Millions, Live in the Caribbean, and Build Wealth by Age 25

by Inaky Strick

"You are the average of the five people you spend the most time with." Over the past few years, I have put Jim Rohn's idea to the test. Since deciding to make a career out of full-time real estate investing, I have made it my mission to find the most successful investors in the business and build relationships with them so that I too could be a successful real estate investor. Putting this idea into action has paid off in more ways than I could have imagined. I now tell people, "Whatever it is you want to do in life, find those who are already successful in doing so and surround yourself with them." This is my story.

My mother worked hard to give me and my younger sister a good life. She expected us to go to school, get a job, work hard, and save money. College came easy for me. I had a lot of fun, joined a fraternity, and became its vice president. I worked full time, paid my own bills, and was able to travel with my friends. I graduated from the McCoy College of Business at Texas State University with good grades and good connections. Everything was aligned perfectly for me to go out and start interviewing with big companies and get a high paying, 9 to 5 corporate job, a "real job."

My last semester in college I took a business elective course that completely changed my path. I chose to take real estate finance for no reason other than that I had to pick an elective and it fit nicely with my schedule. As we started getting into the course, I realized that I truly enjoyed this class and was going above and beyond what was required to get an A. I was reading chapters ahead and started researching real estate outside of the course. I came across a little purple book called *Rich Dad Poor Dad* by Robert Kiyosaki. I had never read a book by choice or for fun, but I ended up reading this book three times in a matter of weeks. Rich Dad Poor Dad became my game changer. Just months before reading this book, I had prepared to schedule interviews for a "real job." Now all that was on my mind was how I could become a successful real estate investor.

I had worked my entire life to prepare to climb the corporate ladder. However, now I wanted to do something that did not require a college education. "My mom would be disappointed." "My college education would be wasted." "What if I am not successful?" These were thoughts going through my head. There was no way to do something different now. It was too easy for me to go get a "real job." The world said I should not become a real estate investor.

After doing some soul searching, I asked myself "What do I want out of life?" I want to travel, spend time with family and give back to those less fortunate. Ultimately, this boils down to freedom. Now knowing what I wanted, it was time to reverse engineer the end goal and figure out how to get there. I wanted a great life, not an average life. If I were to get a "real job," would that put me closer or further away from the goal of being free? Working 9 to 5 in a cubical, five days a week and getting only two weeks of vacation is not what freedom looks like to me. My decision was made. I would become a successful real estate investor.

Now what? This world was completely new to me. Where would I start? Would I continue to work as a waiter to make money to invest? I realized there was more to learn about real estate before investing wisely. I had to figure out a way to make money to invest, support myself, and maximize my time learning about the art of real estate investing. Getting my license to sell real estate was my next logical step. There I was, 23 years old with a college degree. All my friends were out in the corporate world, getting "real jobs" and what was I doing? Studying to take the exam to become a real estate sales agent. Other people who had their license discouraged me, "The test is hard. You won't pass it on the first try." I didn't listen to them. Learning real estate was my new job. And I passed.

If I wanted to be a successful real estate agent, I needed to find those who were already successful, surround myself with them, and spend time with them. My parents had previously sold a house with the best boutique broker in The Woodlands, Texas who had an excellent track record. I asked my parents to invite the broker to our house for dinner. I knew that if I could create a meaningful relationship with the most successful broker in town, I had the chance of becoming like him. We had a good dinner and good conversation. He told me that becoming a great real estate agent was not easy. I believed him, which is why I wanted to work with him.

After getting my license, I asked him for a meeting. I walked into his office, dressed in a brand new suit, big smile on my face with very high confidence. In my head, the job was already mine. I shook his hand and told him, "I am going to work for you." He immediately shut that idea down.

He said "I do not offer training here, you are brand new and have no experience. Go work for Keller Williams for two years. They have excellent training. When you are more experienced, you can come work for me." This destroyed me. This is not how I planned this meeting to go. Keeping a smile on my face and remaining confident, I proceeded to tell him why I would be a valuable asset to his team. I left the meeting with the agreement that he would think about it. He called me back the next day, and we came to an agreement that I could start out by following up with his old leads. These were leads that had not been contacted in years. I took the job because I had to start somewhere, but more importantly, because I would soon be surrounded by the best real estate team in The Woodlands, Texas.

With no luck and no pay, I spent two months following up with these old leads making call after call. Then something magical happened; my mom's friends needed to sell their house, and they wanted to interview me. This was huge. The average sales price in Houston at that point was around $262,000. This property would be listed at $750,000! I didn't want to ask my broker for help because I feared he would make me go into the presentation with another more experienced agent. This would mean the commission would be split. So doing what any normal millennial would do...I went on YouTube and searched "how to do a listing presentation."

I competed against three other experienced agents, but the sellers signed my listing agreement on the spot. A big part of why the sellers chose me to sell their home was based on the fact that I was working with the best brokerage in The Woodlands. This was by far my biggest win ever.

And then there was a sign. I was sitting in the car outside the property feeling like a million bucks, when the song "Shout" by Tears For Fears started playing on my radio. Not having heard this song in years I immediately start crying. My parents divorced when I was young and my mom later remarried. His name was Darrin, and he was there for a big part of my early childhood. He sincerely loved me and my little sister, and we looked up to him. Sometimes we would all pretend like we were in a band; my sister would play air drums, Darrin was the singer, and I played air guitar. "Shout" by Tears of Fears was his favorite song, and we would play it all the time. My junior year in college my mom called me and told me to sit down. I knew something was wrong. Darrin had passed away. This was by far the worst day of my life. When this first big listing agreement was signed and I heard this song, it was a sign that Darrin was watching. I knew at that point that he had my back. I could now do anything because he would always be watching over me. This is when the fear of whether I had made a good or bad decision in my career completely disappeared.

I continued to surround myself with the best: from leading a local, young adults networking organization to appearing as a guest on TV and radio. Opportunities presented themselves one after the other.

One property that I sold had a buyer's agent that worked for the best luxury broker in all of Houston, Martha Turner Sotheby's International Realty. When the transaction closed, she asked if I would like to meet the vice president of Sotheby's. Are you kidding me!? Not even a year into my real estate career, I was invited to sit down with the best broker to work for in all of Houston. The average agent with Sotheby's in Houston sells over seven million dollars of real estate per year. My broker at the time was recognized locally, but Sotheby's could take me international. The vice president asked me to become a Sotheby's agent. The hard part was letting go of my current broker who believed in me when I was just starting out. However, working with Sotheby's International Realty would mean working with more affluent clientele and would put me closer to my end goal of becoming a successful real estate investor. I made the jump to this new opportunity. Working with Sotheby's opened so many doors. I had no trouble securing high dollar listings because of my association with the brand of Sotheby's International Realty. I even got to represent new construction, luxury custom builders. Some of the top agents in my brokerage approached me and asked if I would like to represent these builders with them. At 25 years old, I had the listing agreement for not one, but two custom-built luxury communities. The first community was 12 townhomes on the water starting at $800,000. The second community was going to be 34 homes with a starting price of 1.3 million dollars. These commissions were going to be the biggest checks I would see to date.

While working with Sotheby's, I continued to learn about real estate investing. Even though my real estate sales life was looking pretty good, I wanted to be an investor. I made it a point to surround myself with successful investors by joining local real estate investment associations. Real estate sales were just a vehicle to learn more while generating an income. One day a book on investing in rental properties led me to a podcast *The Real Estate Guys Radio Show* podcast with Robert Helms and Russell Gray. The very first episode I listened to, they were promoting their Investor Summit at Sea. After reading all the details online, I knew I had to be there. The price tag was a little out of my budget, however, being surrounded by the best investors in the business and building relationships would be well worth the price. I sent Robert and Russell a video to apply for their young adults program. I received word that I would be receiving a scholarship that would cut the price in half.

I knew that going to the summit was going to be huge for me, but I had no idea how much it would change my life. On the Investor Summit at

Sea, I met and built relationships with so many of my heroes including Robert Kiyosaki, Tom Hopkins, Ken McElroy, Simon Black, Peter Schiff, G. Edward Griffin, Kyle Wilson, and many more. More importantly, I started a relationship with The Real Estate Guys, Robert Helms and Russell Gray.

During the Summit, we stopped in Belize to visit the most beautiful island, Ambergris Caye. Ambergris Caye is where The Real Estate Guys have their biggest development project to date called Mahogany Bay Village Resort and Beach Club. This is the largest project the entire country of Belize has ever seen. There are four components to the project: the resort which is a Curio by Hilton (the first international brand on the island), the residences which are a "coastal living community" (the first coastal living community outside the US), the townlet, which has restaurants, retail, a yoga studio, a hair salon, a Miami-style pool, and the private beach club (the only private beach on the west side of the island where the sun sets). They sell the resort and residence units to investors. At the end of the nine-day Investor Summit at Sea, The Real Estate Guys asked if I would like to be the leader of the young adults program the following year. Of course, knowing that if I continued to surround myself with the best investors, one day I would be like them, I agreed.

Following the Summit, I had a few phone calls with The Real Estate Guys about creating a business model to bring my clients from Houston down to Belize to check out the investment opportunities. During one of the phone calls, they said, "Hey, what do you think about working directly for us, moving down to Belize and living on site?" This meant I would have to leave Sotheby's and everything that I had worked so hard for. It meant leaving behind the name I had made for myself in Houston. I would leave behind the builders and new construction communities and I would not see any of those big commission checks. I was nervous, but then I remembered that in order to grow as an investor, I needed to surround myself with those who were already successful. I called them back within 45 minutes from the time they had asked me to completely change my life. I said "Robert, Russ...I'm in."

Moving to Belize and learning about the real estate market of Ambergris Caye from Robert Helms, I became the business development manager for Mahogany Bay Village Resort and Beach Club. My job was to know the market, know the product, and find new ways of attracting investors. I did a lot of traveling and presenting in front of large groups of investors. One of my most memorable trips was when I met with Gary Vaynerchuk and our CEO and developer Beth Clifford in New York City. Gary Vaynerchuk is an American entrepreneur, four-time New York Times bestselling author, speaker, internet personality and one of my personal heroes. Securing a meeting with him was not easy. It took me two months and a lot of ass-kissing, but I finally had my 25-minute meeting arranged. The meeting went so well that now Mahogany Bay Village and Gary Vaynerchuk are doing business together. During that trip, we also met with editors from Time Inc.'s different brands including *Money, Fortune, Travel And Leisure, Coastal Living* and many more. After many successes in Belize and living the island life, it was time for me to go back to Texas.

The relationships made on the Investor Summit at Sea continued to pay off. As soon as I posted on Facebook my return to Houston, one of the big-time real estate investors called immediately. He proceeded to tell me his private investment firm, Four Peaks Capital Partners, was growing fast. He said they needed help and wanted me to come on board as the director of investor relations. My primary duties would be to communicate and manage relationships with all current and potential investment partners. Surrounding myself with the right people was paying off bigger than I had expected. I accepted the offer.

I am now learning hands-on from an experienced private real estate investing firm. I am able to help people build wealth by choosing investments backed by tangible, real assets. Our team can provide income and growth through the private real estate investment market to qualified investors. I help people avoid the middleman approach used by Wall Street that charges excessive fees and commissions. All of our investments have little to no correlation to Wall Street or the world markets. Many use this asset class to hedge against inflation and volatility. It feels good to offer investors above-average returns due to the careful selection of investments and streamlined operations. I offer unique access to participate in this asset class that investors may have never had the opportunity to do so as an individual. I am truly working my dream job and on my way to living my dream life!

If you've ever thought that Jim Rohn's saying, "You are the average of the five people you spend the most time with" was a bit cliché, then I challenge you to think again. From going against the status quo of a recent college graduate to living in paradise and now achieving my goal of a career in full-time real estate investing, I can honestly say that this all would not have been possible without surrounding myself with the best. I'm often asked how I was able to achieve exactly what I wanted so fast. My secret is, whatever it is you want to do in life, find those who are already successful in doing so and surround yourself with them.

By the way, I'm just getting started.

TWEETABLE:

Whatever it is you want to do in life, find those who are already successful in doing so and surround yourself with them.

Inaky is a real estate investment advisor. He helps qualified investors build their cash flow and grow their wealth by providing opportunities to invest passively in real estate. His experience extends from investments in single family residences, mobile home parks, and international resort properties. Inaky believes if you want to be successful at anything, you must surround yourself with the best people and teams. To learn more, get free bonuses, and contact Inaky go to www.InakyStrick.com

CHAPTER 5

Tomorrow Is Never Promised

by Stacey LaCroix

I was 17 and ready to embark on the next journey in my life after high school. My neighbor of the same age and I had been friends since we were four, and we had just returned from a night out. We sat in my driveway between our houses until the wee hours of the morning discussing our friendship. I was off to college, while she and several other girls in our group were attending a local business school.

We promised that even though our time together was going to be limited, we would always be there for each other. I had no idea that in that moment... she was really telling me goodbye. This was the last time that I would ever see her, talk to her, and it would become our last hug.

The following Friday, August 12, is a date I will never forget. My friend stopped by my house to invite me to The Old Spaghetti Factory with a few other girls from our group, but I missed her because my best guy friend and I had gone shopping for flowers for his new girlfriend. I was disappointed because they had already left by the time I returned. This was before cell phones, which made communication very difficult. I had previously made plans with another friend. When I got to her house, I found out she had been invited to the Old Spaghetti Factory as well, but couldn't get a hold of me to confirm the change in plans. Since they were already gone, we figured we would meet up with them later. We never ran into our friends, and when I got home, I received the phone call that would change my life forever.

My dear friends were on their way to the bank before heading downtown when traffic backed up. A man, who was driving on a revoked license, came barreling down what was then a two-lane road. He did not realize traffic was backed up to a dead standstill.

He slammed into my friend's car without even touching the brakes, smashing the entire back end. Two of the girls died upon impact. The trailer hitch punctured the gas tank, and the gas began leaking. He continued to push the car across the pavement, and since the back was smashed in, the trailer hitch served as a match scraping against the road. The car burst into flames. My friend in the front seat was desperately trying to escape. A hero several cars back rushed up trying to save them. As he approached the car, he found her reaching for help as the flames crept to the front. When he kicked in the windshield to get her out, the oxygen gave life to the flames, which completely enveloped the car. Three beautiful girls, who had their entire life ahead of them, were taken that night...too tragic...too soon.

This tragedy changed my life forever. I went through the grieving process like everyone else. I was angry, I was sad, I was numb. I no longer wanted to go to college. I remember thinking the three girls were the lucky ones because they were enjoying the pleasures of heaven, while I was down here on Earth enduring the hell of losing them.

I was scared to leave my parents. I feared every time someone would get in a car, they may never come home. I had a difficult time riding with someone else and being a passenger. I always wanted to drive because then I was in control. Anytime someone was late picking me up, I always feared the worst. I lost faith in God and couldn't attend church because all I would do was think about the girls and cry. I watched three families destroyed. I was so angry, and I just couldn't understand why this happened.

As time passed, I knew I had to find a way to continue with my life and attend college. I still don't know why I wasn't home that day. If I had been, there would have been two more of us in that car. I have always wondered if we had been around, could we have changed the timing so that this accident never would have happened...so many what ifs. I don't know why I wasn't in that car, but I knew that I had to accept the fact that life is such a precious gift, and we have to live each and every day like it's our last because tomorrow is never promised.

My friends and I raised money to erect a monument with a gazebo at the high school as a peaceful place of remembrance to represent all of the young lives that were taken way too soon. When I took the proposal to our superintendent, we were still struggling with all the details. I'll never forget how he chastised me in my time of grief as he told me that I was the most disorganized person he had ever met. That didn't stop our mission of creating a memorial to honor our friends. Not only did we raise money for this beautiful setting, we also started a scholarship fund for students who went to the business school that the three girls attended. On the pedestal is a picture of the three girls with the quote, "Remember us with smiles, not tears."

I struggled with my career choice. I felt stuck between accounting because I loved numbers and teaching because I had a passion for children and the process of educating. I started playing school when I was four trying to teach my grandpa. At one point, I told him that he was too stupid to learn. He got the biggest kick out of my sassiness. (Luckily, I became more polished before I became an actual teacher.) My poor little cousins and brother had to endure countless hours of "playing school." Even with the inner-bred teacher in me, I declared accounting as my major when I enrolled in school because I wanted to make money. After this tragedy, my view on life changed. As an accountant, I knew I could make money, but as a teacher, I knew I could make a difference. From that moment forward, I knew I had to make a difference. I wanted to help children and be a positive influence in their lives. I chose to make an impact.

I spent the next 20 years fulfilling that passion. I continued on to get my master's degree in education. I then went through a rigorous program called National Boards, which not only impacted my teaching but also my life. It taught me to be reflective in everything I did so that I could always improve and become better. As I pursued my passion for education, I always had other "jobs" to supplement my income. My dad had instilled in me the work hard, play hard attitude, and I enjoyed staying busy and working. At one time, I worked six jobs that included teaching, coaching cheerleading, teaching an exercise class, bartending, selling real estate and tutoring. After several years of a very intense work schedule, I dropped everything but teaching and real estate and continued to do both professions simultaneously for nine years.

After "No Child Left Behind" was implemented, philosophies in education began to change. The government continued to integrate programs that I personally did not feel were best for children. I was still very passionate about teaching, but I found myself very stressed and struggling to comply with the programs that were being forced into schools. I had always known that I wasn't going to retire as a teacher because I wanted to go out on top, but I wasn't ready to leave after 20 years either. Still, I knew I had to do something, or the stress would start affecting my health.

In addition to my professional struggle, I was dealing with a personal struggle. I had always wanted four children of my own. Circumstances as a result of my choices did not result in that dream. I found myself 40 years old at a crossroad of opting for adoption and becoming a single parent or giving up on the idea of being a parent at all. I knew I couldn't continue real estate and teaching if I wanted to raise a child, but I also financially needed both jobs to do so. The cost of adoption was staggering. I found it very sad that someone made such a business and turned such a profit in finding children a loving home when there are so many people that would make incredible parents, but who don't have the average $40,000 to invest in adoption. I also wrestled with the whether or not I really wanted to be a single parent. I was caught in my internal struggle. *Should I attempt to adopt? Should I leave teaching? Should I stay status quo and continue stressed out working*

70-90 hours per week? As I was searching for answers and dealing with the devastating fact that I may never be able to experience birthing a child, I was introduced to the first network marketing company that had ever sparked my interest.

A former cheerleader I coached called me and said, "You've got to see this business! You'd be great at it!" I was completely disinterested because I was tired of working all the time and definitely did not want to add anything to my plate. She called me eight weeks in a row. Her persistence wore me down, and I finally went to check out this business she wanted me to see. I had no intention of joining, but out of respect, I went to take a look. I was blown away by the business model, and it made sense for me because the services that were offered would complement my real estate business. So I decided to get started. I had no idea how that decision would forever change my life. I never did have children, but dreams in my future will never be limited because of financial resources.

I began my business on a very part-time basis around real estate and teaching. I had some successes, and I had some failures. As I was learning this new business, I continued to struggle with the changes in the teaching profession, but my stress level had reached an all-time high. I kept asking myself, "Are you seriously contemplating a career change at 43? What about all the money you spent on education? How are you going to handle not teaching anymore, especially when it's something you love so much?" If I was going to embark on something new, I had to have a passion for it, and I had to be making a difference.

Thankfully, the company I'm affiliated with feeds hungry children through a food bank program, which as a teacher who watched children go without food, is extremely important to me. I felt I was still making a difference with children. In the network marketing model, you actually have to teach and train people how to do the business effectively, so I was able to continue to teach…just on a different platform. I ultimately made the decision to take a leap of faith and do what was best for my financial future. When I decided to resign from teaching, I told my principal, "I'm not leaving because I lost my passion for teaching, I'm leaving because of my passion for teaching."

I continued selling real estate but had more time to devote to my network marketing business. It's crazy to think of how much I have grown. Even though I've always been comfortable talking in front of children, adults terrified me. When I took my master's classes, there would maybe be 25 adults in the room, and I would never talk unless I was forced. I have since spoken on a stage with hundreds of people. I have learned that when you step out of your comfort zone is when you grow. I now have embraced those times of discomfort, and I welcome them so that I may continue to get better.

I see so many people complain about their life, their job, their weight, their relationship, their financial situation all over social media, but they're never willing to do anything about it. Albert Einstein coined, "The definition of insanity is doing the same thing over and over again and expecting different results." If you're living paycheck to paycheck, how are you going to resolve that problem? If you keep gaining weight but don't change your lifestyle, how can you expect different results? If you have an addiction but don't seek help, how will you ever stop? I have made the choice to surround myself with people who want to be successful, who want to help others, and who choose to be grateful for what they have while continuing to reach for what they truly want, but most importantly who have a passion for life and want to make a difference.

The gentleman who shared this business with me is three-time World Series Champion, Todd Stottlemyre, who is also featured in this book. For the past four years, I have not only developed a business relationship with Todd, but also a friendship with him and his beautiful wife, Erica. They have taught me so much about life, continuing to reach for the stars, and creating balance in my personal life and business. Todd has been an incredible mentor, and I am truly blessed. He has inspired me to be more, to want more, to give more. There are so many lessons in his book, *Relentless Success*, but my favorite quote is, "Anything is possible, the impossible just hasn't been done yet." I am so excited for the future that we're going to create and the lives that we are going to change.

As the co-founder of our company says, "Our business is a professional development program with a compensation plan attached." Even though the residual income has changed my life, the personal development that I have been through helps me continue on the path to staying focused on living with a purpose.

The connections I've made through networking, the dear friends I've made as I have built a business, and the personal growth I have achieved are priceless. I'm forever grateful for every day that I'm blessed with, and look forward to expanding, growing and motivating people to live every day like it's their last because tomorrow is never promised. My goal is that when I leave this Earth, I have touched hundreds of thousands of lives and have truly made a difference.

TWEETABLE

Live every day like it's your last. Life is precious, and tomorrow is never promised. #makeadifference #livewithpurpose

Stacey LaCroix is a former teacher and coach, realtor, professional networker, and entrepreneur. With a master's in education, she continues to use her skills to coach and train people on how to build a business creating residual income. She loves to travel, and her mission in life is to help people from settling and to inspire them to live with passion and purpose all around the world.

https://www.facebook.com/stacey.lacroix.5
https://www.instagram.com/staceylacroix/?hl=en
staceylacroixcoach.com

CHAPTER 6
There's Always a Silver Lining
by Stephen South

I was born in 1982, not far from the sprawling city of Cape Town. It was a tumultuous year in South Africa where the struggle against apartheid continued unabated. The first part of my childhood was spent in the picturesque seaside town of Hout Bay where neighborhoods were segregated into White and Black areas and schools were separated by race.

When I reflect on my early childhood, I realize I led quite a privileged, sheltered life. Our large, thatched, double-story family home looked over an expansive garden where we kept hens and a variety of geese and ducks. My mother, a great cook and keen photographer, was always around. Our house was often filled with music and dancing, great passions of my mom's. Warm, giving, caring, and sensitive, my friends who came to visit and stay over took an instant liking to her. She was my best friend and a soft place to fall. Apart from our two border collies, our house was generally full of stray cats or skinny, sick dogs whom mom had rescued.

My brother and I grew up with parents and grandparents who loved us unconditionally. Sundays involved services at the Baptist church and hikes through the mountains or swims and surfing at the beach. A strong swimmer, my mother spent hours exploring rock pools or swimming with us. She was like a mermaid in the water. My practical, hardworking dad, a mechanical engineer, spent a lot of time in his garage restoring vintage motorbikes or doing maintenance work on our home. He would fix our bikes and skateboards and coach my brother and me how to play cricket.

In the late 80s and towards the end of the apartheid regime, schools started accepting children of all races. My best friend Sydney was the first Black kid to be accepted into my primary school. There could be no greater contrast between my neighborhood than the informal shanty settlement of Imizamo Yethu (Mandela Park) where he lived. Poverty was rampant, and people were living in small shacks without plumbing, electricity, or running water and without roads. Apartheid never made sense to my family. My mother, a supporter of struggle activists in the ANC (African National Congress), welcomed Sydney into our home and encouraged our friendship. Sydney and I had so much fun together playing sports and getting up to loads of mischief! We even started an informal car wash service and earned quite a lot of pocket money. Whenever I visited his humble home, which was very unusual for a young White kid back then, I wondered why there was such a racial divide. Sydney and I felt like brothers.

Initially, my parents enjoyed a relatively happy marriage, but my mother's postnatal depression was never treated properly, and she resorted to alcohol which resulted in many arguments. In many ways, my folks were poles apart and probably shouldn't have married in the first place. At the age of ten, I got the devastating news that they would be separating, which resulted in my mother getting custody of me and my father getting custody of my brother. My dad sold our family home, and I moved with my mother to a small rental cottage closer to my primary school in Hout Bay. This took some adjusting, but with the support of other family members coupled with my passion for sports, I was able to get through this difficult time. I represented my state cricket team throughout my schooling years and always felt complete bliss when I was playing. This was definitely my form of meditation.

Unfortunately, my mother struggled to come to terms with the divorce and continued to drink. Alcohol was her way of coping with her depression and financial difficulties. Although it was immensely distressing and confusing to see the most loving and caring soul turn into a completely different person when she was drunk, I felt a lot of empathy and compassion for her. She was still my mom and best friend. On the other hand, I was very disappointed and often embarrassed when she would pick me up from school or sports practice and it was clear that she had been drinking.

I learned, much later in life, that most of us carry some sort of resentment towards one or both of our parents for not being the parents we wished for. However, I realized that they were doing their best based on their circumstances, coping skills, and upbringing. If they knew better, they would have done better.

Eventually, the stress and harmful effects of drinking caught up with my mom. She had a nervous breakdown and was admitted to a mental institution where she was given electroconvulsive treatment to bring her out of her catatonic state. This was a painful and very challenging period. My mother's sister, my aunt, and I would visit her often. For the first couple of weeks, she didn't even recognize us. At this time I was living with my father and brother in another suburb near my high school. It felt good to be in a structured and stable environment. However, I missed my mom tremendously. She was eventually discharged. After going to various rehab clinics, she went to live with my grandparents.

But life was to dish out some more curve balls for us. Fast forward to 2002. I was 19 and out one night with some of my close friends having drinks at a bar. At around 2am, we decided to head home. As I drove off, I noticed that a crowd of people had gathered in a circle outside the bar we were in. Parking my car, I went to investigate. When I reached the group of people, I could see that paramedics were frantically doing CPR over a body. Then I spotted Cara, the sister of a close friend of mine. She was in hysterics. At that moment my heart sunk. I realized that it was my friend Ryan lying there. The ambulance rushed him to hospital. Tragically, he died the next morning after his life support was switched off. Apparently, he had been crossing the road when a driver went through the red light and ran him over. He was a gifted student with the world ahead of him. It took years for his family to come to terms with his death.

Then two months later, on Christmas Eve, I was lying in bed with my girlfriend when my father knocked frantically on my bedroom door, screaming for help. His new long-term partner, a gifted teacher, a mother of two, had collapsed on the floor shortly after having had an argument with her thirteen-year-old daughter. Adele had a history of suicide attempts and depression but had been stable for quite a long while. We were concerned she had taken an overdose of pills, so we rushed her to the hospital. Within fifteen minutes, the doctor pronounced her dead. We discovered later that she had swallowed mole poison. My father and I then had to gather the strength to give the horrific news to her daughters and mother.

A few weeks later, I was playing in a cricket match and had just come off the field when I was met by my brother Joshua. He informed me that my mother had been diagnosed with stage four terminal cancer. At this stage, it felt like I was living in a nightmare and I would wake up soon and everything would be back to normal. Unfortunately, that never happened. I had to come to terms with the fact that my beloved mother would also be leaving me.

As she didn't have medical insurance, my aunt and I took her to a government hospital on a weekly basis where she initially had chemotherapy. They would also give her blood transfusions and drain fluid from her swollen stomach. It felt as though I had entered a grey world of suffering. Towards the end of her life, my aunt rented a cottage for my mom in Hout Bay. It was on the slopes of a cliff face, right near the sea. My mother had a deep passion for the sea. I slept next to her, breathing in the smell of the ocean, listening to the soothing sound of waves and seagulls. With the help of hospice and morphine to relieve her discomfort, she was able to laugh and joke with her close friends and other family members. One very special day, my dad visited. He had brought along some family photograph albums. Bit by bit, the bitterness and acrimony melted away.

They made peace with each other. Four months after her diagnosis she passed away peacefully on Mother's Day. We had to break the news to my brother who had just arrived from London.

I remember that day so clearly—the urgent need to have some time on my own. I walked down to the seashore, sat on a rock, and prayed. I implored God to give me answers. Why had I lost the closest person in my life at such a young age as well as two other very close people all within the space of six months?

Then, after a long silence, a voice came into my head...Stephen, you have two choices here. Either you decide to feel sorry for yourself and have a victim attitude or you turn the worst possible negative into the biggest possible positive. I decided from that moment, no matter what life threw at me from that point onwards, nothing could be worse than losing my mother. That realization immediately lifted me with an incredible amount of strength. I felt an intense amount of gratitude for the love and kindness my mother had given me throughout my life, as this taught me how to truly love and be kind to others.

Shortly after her passing, I realized that I needed a change of environment. My father paid for me to do a short programming course at a local computer school. It had always been a dream of mine to live and work in London. After doing various odd jobs, I managed to save enough money for a flight plus an extra £1,000 which was to last me until I got a job. Three weeks after arriving in London at the age of 21 I was literally down to my last £20. I had been on numerous unsuccessful interviews and was feeling despondent and discouraged. I dreaded the thought of having to call my father and ask for a bailout. Then my cell rang. It was Sanjay from one of the recruiting agencies I had registered and interviewed with. I still remember his words. "Steve, I'm afraid we still haven't been able to find you a software engineer position. However, we think you would make a great software engineering recruiter." I had never thought of becoming a recruiter, but the more I thought about it, the more it made sense. I realized that my heart wasn't into becoming a software engineer, but I thoroughly enjoyed interacting and dealing with people. Plus, the technical knowledge I had acquired gave me a huge advantage over most other recruiters.

After working five very productive years at a well-known recruiting company, I decided to set up my own company with one my colleagues. Before we knew it, we were fast becoming one of the most respected IT recruiting agencies in London. After ten years in London, my British girlfriend (now wife) and I decided we needed a change and agreed that Los Angeles presented the perfect location for both of our careers, and it ticked a very important box for us...the weather! Two years later I sold my shares in the company and traveled to LA to set up a similar company called Source Coders.

Shortly afterwards, I hit a big stumbling block as I found myself waking up feeling uninspired. After some intensive soul searching, I realized that in order to move forward, I needed to contribute in a more positive, meaningful way. I had more to offer than just finding people the highest paying job. As a result, I began working with companies and candidates who were committed to making a positive, ethical, and meaningful impact in the world.

I have always dreamed of starting a charity for underprivileged children and orphans in Africa and realized that I had to make this a reality. Today, fortunately, technology is empowering ordinary people with information to rise above poverty and do extraordinary things. I was given a head start when I was a child and now it is my turn to give back.

Recently, I set up a non-profit named Head Start Children's Foundation. Along with three of my closest childhood friends, we plan to expose children in developing countries to a variety of learning opportunities that they normally would not have access to. Subjects and activities will include extramural sports, arts, music, pottery, technology, coding, yoga, prayer, meditation, and more. Once they have found their passion, the next phase is to nurture and support them to start a career within this field. We plan to teach them spiritual principles as well such as gratitude, visualization, the law of attraction, the power of affirmations, and all the amazing skills that educate a child in ways to think, speak, and become a leader. We are in the planning phase of launching our first centre in Cape Town. Our long-term vision is to replicate these centres throughout Africa and Asia and wherever else in the world there is a need for them.

Although I often have moments of doubt that I'm not capable of pulling off such a feat, I've learned that in order to grow, we have to embrace the discomfort. Having lived through terrible pain and loss, I have no fear of seeking to accomplish all of the great things I desire, and I want to help people who lack the opportunities I have had. If your intention is strong enough, the universe and God will always work in your favor to help you achieve your dreams!

TWEETABLE

I often have moments of doubt, but I've learned that in order to grow, we have to embrace the discomfort.

Stephen South is an entrepreneur, bestselling author, and philanthropist.

He is the founder of Source Coders, a leading software engineering staffing firm which focuses on connecting purpose driven coders with organizations that are making a difference. He is also the founder of Head Start Children's Foundation a non-profit that helps underprivileged children in Africa by teaching them how to think and find their true passion in life.

stephen@sourcecoders.io
www.sourcecoders.io
https://www.instagram.com/sourcecoders
www.headstartfoundation.org

CHAPTER 7

Insecure Farm Kid Learns from Andy

by Matt Byler

I stared at Andy's back, bewildered. What on Earth had just happened?

But wait. Let me start at the beginning.

I was in Florida for volleyball playoffs. What an absolute pleasure! While my remote valley in Pennsylvania was in the icy grips of winter, for one short week my friends and I were in the sun and sand of the paradise called Florida. And there was so much to do!

Who will I meet today? Wow, she is cute! I wonder if she likes me...

I wonder if she will even notice me....

Along with all the girls were all the guys. The competition was strong, as we all tried to outdo each other, burning through our meager savings at an alarming rate. In Florida, you could only wear the best clothes, have perfect hair, and drive unbelievably shiny vehicles. New wheels were a wise investment before heading South. I worked out trying to fill my shirt a bit more and trying to jump just a little higher. Although I did my best, the unfortunate truth was all the other guys did those things, too. And I could barely keep up. Like I said, the competition was brutal.

This was in those tough years between childhood and adulthood. My body had beat my mind to the maturity line. I struggled a lot with low self-esteem.

On the court, the victories were hollow in my mind because who I had beaten simply wasn't all that good. Or I would think a great opponent made a mistake which allowed me to win. I know! It was a vicious circle with no good exit point.

I had made a valuable discovery that year, though. I discovered that if I acted condescending and cold, people would appear to be intimidated. This was wonderful! It was a new freedom that I treasured.

Even cool kids would become unsure and edgy! All I needed to do was to be careful to look and act the part. I chose my friends carefully to help maintain the image.

I was cool. Period.

At least on the outside. Not so much on the inside.

Inside, I was still the same guy. I still didn't like myself. I wanted friends, but I didn't want them to know me too well. After all, if they got to see the real me, how could they like me?

One evening we were at a gym to play volleyball. At the moment I was off the court, waiting until it was my turn to play again.

I was sitting by a wall watching the on-court teams play, just evaluating the players. Some were really outstanding. Hopefully, I wouldn't need to face up against them. My weaknesses would then be apparent in short order.

I was practicing my cool, confident look. What a relief to see kids look jumpy and ill-at-ease when our eyes met. It was working!

Suddenly a lanky form caught my eye. It was a fellow that I hadn't seen in four years. His name was Andy. I remembered him well because he had a sister that was beautiful. And whattaya know, there he was. Of all the kids in the gym, Andy was certainly the worst dressed. He was 6'2" and skinny. His clothes were so badly out of style. And his hair! Unbelievable! I felt sorry for him. He had to feel terrible.

One thing for sure, I could not be seen talking to him. I watched him talk to unfortunate kids that he cornered as he made his way through the gym.

Then, he saw me. I saw the recognition in his eyes as he headed straight towards me. Oh no! I couldn't get away now without being rude. I waited, cringing.

"Matt! How are you doing?"

What? He remembered my name! And I didn't have a sister to help me stand out.

"Uh, good," I said. "You look familiar. You are...Andy?" Inside I was saying, Just go. Please! Now.

"Yes!" he said, beaming. "Welcome to Florida!" He shook my hand enthusiastically. "When did you get here?"

"Oh, it was the day before yesterday." I muttered.

"Well, I hope you enjoy your stay! And if you're here on Sunday, come to my church. It's good to see you again!" And he was off.

I watched him walk away and greet someone else just as enthusiastically. The person he was talking to looked at him and smiled while they visited. Then he talked to another. And another.

Boy, I like Andy, I thought as I watched him go. Suddenly I realized what I had just thought.

What? I had just been thinking he is a dork, even embarrassed for him, and now I had just thought that I like him....

I focused on him more closely. Everyone appeared happy to see him, really happy even. Their faces would light up. Their mouths would go, "Andy!" He would shake each hand, maybe clap a shoulder, visit for a bit, and keep going. And then the kids' faces would go back to normal.

I stared at Andy's back, bewildered. What on Earth had just happened? I was so much cooler than Andy in pretty much every way possible, and yet no one lit up like that when I came by.

What I really wanted was to have friends. That was the true reason for putting so much effort into my cars, my clothes, and my game. By all appearances, Andy wasn't worried about any of these.

And yet he had 10 friends to my one.

I sat there without moving for a very long time. I was deep in thought. Here was a secret of life that I had to unlock.

As I sat there that evening, and as I went running on the beach the next morning at sunrise, I was pondering.

I slowly realized that although opposites, both low self-esteem and high self-confidence were "self"-ish. They were all about me. Andy was neither. He was others focused. By all appearances, he took no thought for himself at all. It was almost like he forgot about himself.

Because of how he made others feel he received all the love and friendship that I wished for. He had developed a much better path to his results.

It's a little weird to compare a person to a dog, but I adore my dog. Andy was like my dog. My dog is always thrilled to see me. He doesn't worry if his hair is perfect. He worries that I'll get home and he'll miss my entrance. He doesn't expect anything in return for welcoming me. My welcome is his goal.

Even so, in return for his attention, I always take the time to hold his head in my hands and rub it for a bit while talking to him. And he wriggles all over with joy.

My dog has neither high self-confidence nor low self-esteem. My dog is unaware of himself. He is focused on me!

And I really like my dog. Just because of that.

Since that day I have tried to welcome others, to make them feel wanted and important. I still often feel shy and insignificant, but I am aware that it doesn't matter how I feel. What matters is how I make others feel.

When I make others feel important, they respond in a like manner which creates happier feelings than I have ever gotten by focusing on myself.

This works in business too. When I help people to gain stable, long-term, passive income, they are freed to spend more time with their families rather than being a slave to their jobs. The better I can serve them the more likely they are to return for more, which increases my deal flow and allows me to serve them even better.

In marriage, when I put my wife's interests ahead of my own, it is natural for her to respond in kind. Then it is yet easier for me to be nice, and the happy cycle continues.

Children are no different. When I truly care for them, they are calmer and more obedient. Who doesn't like happy, obedient children? Especially when they are your own! And then it is easier to be patient, and then they feel more secure....

When I focus on getting the result I want, I am focused on getting.

When I first give what I desire, it becomes much more likely that I will get what I want. But it is not about getting. It is about giving. Until I can forget about myself, life is difficult.

When I serve humbly, when all my joy is in you; life blossoms! When life happens and people are disagreeable, the root of the problem is always that I was focused on getting rather than giving.

The cycle, good or bad, begins with me.

Giving is a source of true joy that getting can never compare to.

Winston Churchill once said: "We make a living by what we get. We make a life by what we give."

There is a similar scripture verse. "It is more blessed to give than to receive." Acts 20:35

I was aware of this Bible verse since I was a child. But I never fully understood it until I saw Andy act it out.

This experience was one small thing that truly changed everything for me!

But wait, there's more!

In the years since then I have also discovered that when I can partner with people who have that "others focused" attitude, my life gets massively easier and better.

Finding those partners has been like bolting a supercharger on an engine. It has transformed my life.

It has made business deals both much more pleasant and profitable.

Even in elite, world-class, investing groups it applies.

It has made 12 years of marriage a source of happiness.

This principle has allowed me to go from an insecure, unhappy farm kid with an 8th grade education to a fulfilled business owner and investor. I have multiple businesses and am in the top 1% of earners. I am part of several elite, high level, investment groups. I have a wife and five children that I really, really like. I treasure my friends and neighbors. There are several businesses that pay me to coach them.

Of course, the money is important. But without the people, the money would (1) not have happened (2) be irrelevant. And neither the people nor the money would be present if I had not first learned to care about others.

I never dreamed I could have this much success. Or friends!

And it is not because of me. It is because of what Andy taught me.

Although I haven't seen Andy in the years since that evening, his lesson has remained.

Thanks, Andy!

TWEETABLE

Giving is a source of true joy that getting can never compare to.

Matt Byler is a husband, father, entrepreneur, and real estate investor/syndicator. He currently has several six- and seven-figure businesses, holdings in agricultural, residential, multi-family, and resort sectors both domestic and international.

He is passionate about helping others to find both financial freedom and their mission on earth, and directing profits to Kingdom focused ministries.

Facebook: Matt Byler
Email: matt@investorsoasis.com
Website: www.learninvestretire.com
Phone: 570-847-8686

CHAPTER 8

The One Day Sabbatical

How Four Questions Created a Six-Figure Residual Income

by Frank Mulcahy

My professional and speaking career started when I first met Larry Thompson and Jim Rohn in 1982. I quickly related to their teachings and looked at them as my mentors and heroes. So many of their lessons helped me succeed in untold abundance during those early years. One of those lessons, which I held within me but never tested for almost 30 years, changed my life when I was at my lowest point. It was critical in helping me create the massive success I have today. I would like to share with you exactly how I discovered the critical importance of taking a "successful sabbatical" even if it's only one day.

I got involved with Herbalife back in '82 when Larry Thompson was the VP of training. I started making a lot of money with them, but I decided to leave multi-level marketing in 1986 after Herbalife had problems with the Food and Drug Administration. Fate would have it that I received a call from Larry Thompson in '98, we did a couple of projects together, and it was then that I had additional contact with Jim Rohn. Larry and Jim deserve all the credit for teaching me a set of skills that helped shape my belief tapestry on life. I didn't know until I had to use these lessons how important they would be in putting me back on track for residual wealth in a new field at a critical time 26 years later.

My lifelong goal was to retire by age 50, so in June 2001 I retired on my 50th birthday. My wife Lynne and I sold our Texas homes and moved back to New Hampshire. We were able to purchase our dream home, 6500 square feet, 26 wooded acres, 7-acre private pond, and simply beautiful. It wasn't long before I got bored with retirement, so I started buying investment properties. My plan was to collect rent, change light bulbs, go fishing, let the property appreciate, and build a legacy for our children. I was up to 57 rental units when the economy crashed along with the housing bubble. I was losing everything I owned, in total I lost almost five million dollars in value, along with my pride, my inspiration, but not my belief system. I never had any doubt I could succeed again especially in the great land we live in called America. As Jim always said, "They don't build boats to go to Cuba." I always believed that this was the greatest land for opportunity, if we are ready to work hard and seize the opportunities we have.

I was searching for something special I could do, something that I could be proud of, something that provided real value to the consumer. That's when the Lord brought me to the company I work with now, Prepaid Legal - LegalShield. Today people see my success and they think, he must have had it easy. They believed I had lots of connections, associations, and a huge database. What I actually had was a deep unshakeable belief system that in America we can achieve whatever we set out to do. As Larry said to me once, "You have never not achieved your goal, unless you quit pursuing it."

It wasn't easy starting over at age 57, moving back to Texas, broke and out of resources. I also realized quickly that the job market after 40 is extremely difficult. Many of you know people looking for something to grab on to, something to believe in, something that can change the rest of their lives.

I hoped this opportunity in employee benefits, identity theft training, and seminars would be our answer. Because of the mounting debt, I was not 110% committed. In the first 90 days, I made less than $1,900. So, I was going to quit. But I couldn't do it once my incredible wife and best friend since 1980 said, "I have never known you to quit anything, so why now?"

Lost, not knowing what I was going to do at 57, unemployable in the down economy, and going further in debt, I went back to the early journals that I kept from my teachings with Jim and Larry. In my notes, I found the simple strategy that, once implemented, dramatically changed my life. The key lessons involved a sabbatical and four powerful questions that needed to be asked and answered in honesty.

It was time for a "serious day-long sabbatical." I took a couple of yellow pads, found privacy, and had a real hard, serious talk with myself. I had to look at things the way they truly were, not how I wanted them to be. I didn't want to put my head in the ground like an ostrich. I had to ask those tough questions. It was a process, the same process that Larry taught me years earlier. I can tell you now that because I followed this process, I was able to, in less than nine months, create a solid six-figure income that now is a multi-six figure RESIDUAL income. This sabbatical allowed me to implement a "proven, repeatable process" with full confidence and belief that I could succeed again with the few resources I had inside myself.

In the sabbatical process, I focused on four questions from an early lesson I heard from Jim Rohn, "The Four Ifs." Amazingly, I had that lesson within me for almost 36 years, but I never had to put it to the test. It was this one strategy that, when my back was against the wall, came to me clearly. I want to share with you the process I went through. Hopefully it is helpful to someone you know.

Question 1: What if I learn?

What if I take the time to stop and learn about the opportunity I have in front of me?

I asked myself, what could I do if I really, truly studied what was ahead of me? I saw all the successes of others, but I really didn't understand that opportunity.

After rigorous and careful study, I had the vision and was in a position where I knew with unwavering confidence that I had found the right company. The founder had outstanding character, the opportunity and compensation plan are unparalleled, and the product is of the highest-quality and not replicable. There was also great demand for the service, no competition, no inventory to store, no capital investment, and the possibility of a lifetime of residual income. And my initial investment was less than $200.

Question 2: What if I try?

What if I actually gave 110% effort in the program? I'm not talking about a half-baked, lukewarm attempt. What if I implemented a daily, weekly, monthly method of operation? If I implemented it, how far could I stretch? How far could I take my talent? How far could I go if I shared this process with others?

I remember Jim said he was talking to some second graders one day. As he set up a two-foot bar, he asked them if they thought they could jump over it. Some said yes, others no, others didn't know. Jim asked them, "Well, how do you know unless you try? If you knock it over, try a second run, and another, and another."

Jim put a word with the word "try." He would say try it UNTIL. That one simple word has stuck with me since the first time I heard Jim Rohn say it.

We don't stop a baby from trying when they fall learning how to walk. We just laugh, we encourage and we say, nice try. Now try it again, and again, until they walk. " Go out there. Talk to your associates, talk to your customers, talk to your upline. But you keep trying, and you keep trying "UNTIL."

Another lesson was from Larry Thompson. "The heavy chains of worry are always forged in idle hours." In other words, if we get busy, productive, and stick to it, the problems of life will just disappear and be replaced with success.

Question 3: What if I stay?

What if I stayed for 1000 days? Now, 1000 days may initially sound like a big commitment, but when you're talking about your life, your career, your retirement, 1000 days is a very short window.

I would break it into segments. 90 days to establish my momentum. Then 90 days to maintain my momentum. Then a third set of 90 days to advance my momentum. Then simply repeat it again and again until you get the results that you desire.

Question 4: What if I care?

Jim always said, "If you care a little, you'll get some results. If you care enough, you'll get incredible results."

That's the posture that my wife and I take to the marketplace. We care more about the results the customers get from our products than the money we make selling them. We care more about the success of the associates we bring into this business than the money we make from those associates. I will share with you that if you'll develop that same philosophy, that same pride, where you can go out there and care the way we have, you can have this kind of success.

Those four questions started me on the path to becoming crystal clear, but those four questions were just the beginning. Following the lessons of my mentors, I evaluated everything in my life. What was working? What wasn't working? Who was helping me succeed? Who was holding me back?

Because I was thorough, thoughtful, and complete in the process, my success skyrocketed. The result was that I was able to make a significant six-figure income in nine months and went on to make double six-figure incomes in residual income over the next couple of years. Residual income is a lot different from regular sales income. In today's economy, it's so hard to find the right combination of sales and recruiting. I did in network marketing what most people didn't do. I did it off my own efforts, not the efforts of thousands. I knew I could depend on myself and a proven process with the right belief system. That was the belief system Jim and Larry shared with me 36 years ago, and it works even better today.

My company has a book called *Profiles of Success*. These stories are written by people who are highly accomplished, and they invited me to contribute my story. The Founder, Mr. Harland Stonecipher called me and said, "You and Lynne have a story people need to hear. When you were knocked down on your knees, you took things and changed your life without complaining. You just went to work and did it. That is an incredible skill that a lot of people need to know they too may have."

After the book was published, Mr. Stonecipher invited me to speak at the company's 2010 annual convention. They brought in all the high income earners, the board of directors, 200 attorneys, and put them in the first thirty rows. Incredibly, I was only in the business for a year and I was asked to go on stage addressing 17,000 people. It was a scary assignment, until I actually started speaking, never looking at my notes. The belief system Jim and Larry shared with me allowed me to speak from the heart naturally. Jim always said if it is in your heart, you will be able to deliver the message.

It was the most incredible experience I ever had because so many people were able to relate to my journey. After I spoke, I had 600-700 people approach me the rest of that weekend and asked me to either take a photo, sign their book, or just talk to them for a moment. They were so grateful that I was able to share with them that no matter how bleak things look, if we can just take a little bit of time, study the things that help us and those things that hurt us, and lay out a plan, our whole lives can change.

But the incredible thing was that even though I touched their hearts, they did more for me in return. See, they reaffirmed that my belief system was right on track. Helping and serving others will always benefit us in the end.

I want to let others know that the journey I took is totally duplicatable. It's a repeatable, proven process that can put anybody onto a fast track of success no matter what they do in life, whether they are interested in my opportunity or anything else. I think some of you after hearing this will be interested in joining me.

A quote from Helen Keller says it best. "Sometimes the most beautiful things in the world cannot be seen or heard but can only be felt in the heart."

That's what my business and my company mean to my wife and me.

Find your dream. Take a sabbatical and ask yourself "The Four Ifs."

Thank you to Jim Rohn and Larry Thompson for having such an impact on my life.

TWEETABLE
Take an honest sabbatical. Ask yourself the hard questions and look at how things truly are, not how you want them to be.

Frank Mulcahy is an author, speaker, coach, and employee benefits broker who has developed public speaking and corporate workshops exposing the risk and devastating cost of ID theft. His "proven, repeatable process" benefits companies by "reducing risk, reducing operating cost, and increasing profits." This is accomplished at "no capital expense" to the company. He is currently looking for others to share his Proven Repeatable Blueprint. Join our team, allow us to help you develop a lifetime of residual income.

fmulcahy@MulcahyAssoc.com
Twitter @FJMulcahySr
www.MulcahyAssoc.com
www.linkedin.com/in/frank-mulcahy-sr-044b267

CHAPTER 9

How I Found Success as a Passionate Real Estate Investor and Intrapreneur by Age 24

by Jennifer Zhang

Being honest with myself would have saved a lot of time that I could have used to do what I actually wanted to do.

I had just graduated from UCLA with degrees in art and anthropology, not knowing what to do with my life. My gallery internships in college were unfulfilling, yet I found myself applying for full-time positions at the same galleries that I couldn't even stand working 10 hour weeks at. If I failed, my parents would get to say, "I told you so" about studying something more practical. Honestly, I had burned out from art, but I was afraid to admit it.

I wish I were honest with myself much earlier. I felt pressured to stick to art because people told me I was talented and creative. Art was the passion or hobby activity people wished they could be doing. For me, it was completely academic. I spent 14 years of year-round classes, up to 50-hour weeks in the summer, in a studio that taught a right and wrong way to make art, resulting in various awards, including the United Nations Art for Peace award, newspaper and television appearances, and my precious college application portfolio.

While my journey with art taught me a lot, there was a thin line between quitting prematurely when things got hard and sticking to it for the wrong reason.

I took a position with a multi-level sales company.

If you want to go fast, go alone. If you want to go far, go together.
– African proverb

I saw this quote every day in our lobby.

In this business, I was introduced to entrepreneurship and financial freedom. I was also introduced to Robert Kiyosaki's books, where I learned the distinction between solopreneurs and business owners. I realized that there was no exit in this business.

At my peak, I had 15 full-time team members. Instead of my business becoming more automated, I found myself interviewing four hours every weekday to offset high turnover, training new hires in the field, training trainers how to train, while still being on the sales floor myself. Every top manager was still involved in their business daily.

I wasted more time being inauthentic with myself. I went fast and ended up alone.

Sales 101 and NLP courses taught me the "how" of being a people person: the eye contact, body language, and what to say. I became skilled at pretending to build rapport with customers who I saw as moneybags and pretending to care about my trainees' goals when I cared more about my team headcount. I was likable, but had shallow relationships.

I was in such denial. I was crying daily. I dreaded the 60-hour weeks of being told "no." Yet the glamor of being my own boss and fear of being a quitter kept me going. So I kept hiring, selling, and building my team to rush to the end destination: personal recognition.

A year later, I finally qualified for the big promotion and relocated to Phoenix. Only one of fifteen team members followed me there, and I was unsuccessful rebuilding my team. I quit after six months, justifying my choice by blaming the nature of the company.

Again, not being honest with myself stopped me from finding what I wanted. I went fast, and I ended up alone.

Because I didn't learn from my mistake, I repeated it with an art collector I met in Scottsdale. His Wall Street background, deep knowledge of art, and having both capital and inventory seemed the perfect complement to my art background, sales, and management skills. We moved to Beverly Hills to start an art auctioneer. I learned about flipping Old Masters paintings and applied systems from the sales business to start a scalable business from scratch. We had only met a month before starting the business, and we soon discovered a number of incompatibilities. I also realized that I had no idea how to run a business. I quit, blaming him and the company while hiding my true intention that this was supposed to be my ticket to success.

I was still attached to making it as an entrepreneur. The next step I took from flipping high-end paintings was spending $60k on high-interest credit cards for house flipping seminars, justifying my investment with doing my first deal before the 0% APR expires.

I jumped two feet in. I formed an entity, mailed letters, knocked on doors, and actively attended local investment clubs. I found a mentor who taught me everything about wholesaling properties and…repeated my pattern of running away and blaming everything but myself when things got tough.

I couldn't keep avoiding how much I was depending on my entrepreneurship "working out" because I could no longer pay my rent. I had a choice to keep living this predictable cycle or to take responsibility.

My pride prevented me from seeking traditional employment or asking my parents for help this whole time, but I was too deep in debt. I moved home and got a job.

The sales company ingrained in me that employees were losers and business owners were successful. The biggest limiting belief I overcame was that being an employee meant I was a sell-out.

I wish I learned what an intrapreneur was earlier. An intrapreneur, or inside entrepreneur, is someone who behaves like an entrepreneur within a larger organization.

I found a job I loved as an intrapreneur working for a real estate entrepreneur. I got free mentorship while receiving a paycheck instead of paying for expensive mentorship. I could contribute more than I could have individually by leveraging an existing brand and its followers to make a bigger impact on more people in less time.

My purpose in life is being authentic with myself and connecting with people.

Starting a business often isn't about inventing the most revolutionary thing. Many of the most successful businesses are not new ideas; they're successful because they're able to impact more lives more deeply.

The missing piece behind my attempts at starting businesses was that I was in it for me. It hit me really hard when I finally discovered that I did not actually care about my customers and team members, even though I talked and acted like I did. It was evident when only one out of fifteen people followed me to start my business in Phoenix. I would tell people that I was working to get time and money freedom for myself and my family when I really just wanted admiration.

I discovered that money is not the destination. It's a vehicle, and it's not the only vehicle. Relationships, experiences, and knowledge are all valuable vehicles. My circumstances, income, accomplishments, and failures did not define me. From this discovery, my life became about being present to the journey, rather than focusing only on the destination.

My choice to be interested in others profoundly impacted every area of my life. It made boring speakers at seminars engaging, and it helped me remember names and details about people. I noticed that people felt heard, understood, and deeply connected around me.

I also recognized that failing doesn't make me a failure. I didn't realize that I had a choice about what my failures meant to me. So instead, I made my failures mean that I was successful because the victory was the action of having taken a risk, not the result.

I made moving home mean that I was a loser, to the point where I was avoiding friends, and certainly avoiding dating. Over the year, I created adult relationships with my mother, my teen brother, and father who lives in China. I had never been closer to my brother, who I had almost no contact with since I went to college. I became reconnected to the high academic pressure school environment I grew up in.

My brother got me involved in teen mental health advocacy. From my journey, I felt compelled to share my message that *your college major doesn't determine your life!* Each person's journey is unique. There is no such thing as "getting life right the first time," and the pursuit of it is not worth compromising mental health, relationships, and self-esteem.

I started liking living at home, and when I *owned* living at home, the shame disappeared. Within a year, I got engaged to the love of my life!

Now having an income and no overhead costs, I started cleaning up my finances. My credit score dropped by 250 points in the six months I took out $60k on credit cards, and my 0% APR period had ended. I saved aggressively, paid off my debt, fixed my credit, moved out of my parents' house, and invested in two commercial properties in 2017.

Without limiting beliefs, my life became limitless.

Today, I raise money from high net worth investors for commercial real estate syndications. Being a young Asian woman is atypical in my industry. Instead of seeing it as a setback, I fully leveraged my identity and was able to grow our client base significantly while reducing overhead costs through creating marketing targeted to Chinese American investors, developing our online presence, and hiring virtual assistants.

In 2017, I founded the Bay Area Commercial and Multifamily real estate investment club, where we educate investors of all experience levels on how to advance to the big leagues of real estate investing.

I always liked the idea of speaking and coaching because I love empowering people, but felt I didn't have enough life experience to be effective. When I distinguished that age wasn't a direct translation of experience or wisdom, I saw what I needed to do: learn and practice. I have gotten incredible leadership, professional, and personal development training at Landmark Worldwide, which has transformed my life and given me the skill to choose how life occurs to me (a common theme you may have noticed in this story).

By letting go of feelings of unworthiness and low self-esteem, I had room for love and contribution. There is no age, gender, or ethnic requirement to practice giving and receiving love generously. Coming from not saying "I love you" growing up, I am so grateful for my breakthrough in expressing love to all people, especially to the closest people in my life. My purpose shifted from being self-focused to being of service to others when I truly recognized the ripple effect of my actions on other people. That is my secret to finding success in my life at 24 years old.

TWEETABLE
Going from entrepreneur to employee is not selling out. As an intrapreneur working for a successful entrepreneur, I make a bigger impact on more people in less time.

Jennifer Zhang is a real estate investor and manages marketing, operations, and Chinese client relations at a Silicon Valley real estate investment firm. Founder of the Bay Area Commercial and Multifamily investment club (www.BACOMM.club), Jennifer is a former entrepreneur with a background in fine art and sales. She is passionate about helping all people, especially young people, realize how powerful they are. To discuss collaboration, contact her at fb.me/TheJenZhang.

CHAPTER 10

Evidence of Success
by Robert Helms

"You don't have to give natural childbirth to ideas. You can adopt them."
– Bob "The Godfather of Real Estate" Helms

As we took our seats in the hotel ballroom, it seemed like a typical gathering of real estate agents, lenders, and related service providers. Our office manager was a big believer in these types of events, and I had been to quite a few. Usually I met new people, took a few notes, got motivated (for at least a few days), and looked for some slice of wisdom that I could apply to my real estate sales career.

Little did I know, in eight hours my life would never be the same.

A good friend and fellow agent told me a week earlier, "You HAVE to see this guy." Yet when I asked why, she couldn't articulate a compelling argument. "It's hard to explain. You'll see."

When he hit the stage, the first thing I noticed about the man, who would turn out to become one of my primary mentors, was that he wasn't a natural speaker. Don't get me wrong, he had terrific energy and passion. But many real estate gurus who rolled through town were polished and practiced. This guy was all over the place. But unlike many of the others I'd seen, it was obvious that he was sharing what he actually did to get business in a very competitive space rather than just spouting off ideas that sounded good in theory.

You see, Walter Sanford was one of the top agents in the state at the time and would go on to be the top-earning agent in the United States for many years. And he didn't speak for a living. He sold real estate. Lots of it. One or two times a month he'd travel to another city and share what was working for him.

He shared over 80 ideas with us that day. Marketing ideas. Lead generation ideas. Client service ideas. Referral ideas. Time and cost saving ideas. My head was spinning. I was excited and terrified at the same time. It seemed like so much!

And then he shared a piece of wisdom that would help me implement some of these great ideas. He explained that many agents would get so worked up after a day like this that they would attempt to change everything about their business overnight. These agents, he said, would most likely fail.

His advice was to go down the list of ideas we planned to implement and pick just one or two. Not a dozen. Not even four. One or two. That way we would have a much better chance of succeeding in our implementation. And once we had mastered one or two—only then should we attempt to add another.

And he was so right.

Step by step, idea by idea, we started to make changes in our real estate sales business. My dad Bob (we call him The Godfather of Real Estate) was already a successful broker. By adding some of Walter's ideas, we went on to place in the top 1% of agents in our company worldwide.

So clearly, the ideas worked. However…it wasn't the ideas that made the difference that day. It was my belief that change was possible.

You see, the big "aha" for me was really quite simple. To make it in real estate, we didn't have to reinvent the wheel, work 14 hour days, or dream up some killer marketing idea that had never been done. Rather, we just had to follow in the footsteps of someone who came before.

We needed to model ourselves off of someone who had been there, done that (both well and poorly), and figured it out. Walter had done the hard work. We just had to follow his lead.

How would we do this? The notes I took would be just the beginning. See, Walter had taken the time to document his systems. He had great checklists to be sure we'd know exactly what to do and not have to rely on memory. He put together a book of the very best letters and communication he used, so we had templates. He scripted many of the key points he made during listing and offer presentations. A modest investment in these materials returned handsomely.

But my dad and I didn't stop there. We continued to seek knowledge from people who were operating at a higher level than we were—in real estate, sales, customer service, investing, and personal development. We read, watched, and studied Tom Hopkins, Brian Tracy, Terri Murphy, Og Mandino, David Knox, Connie Podesta, Michael Gerber, Stephen Covey, Joe Stumpf, Anthony Robbins, Floyd Wickman, Bonnie St. John, Zig Ziglar, Brian Buffini, Denis Waitley, Robert Kiyosaki, and of course, Jim Rohn. And with the belief that if they could do it, we could do it…we did.

Success leaves clues.

This lesson has followed me throughout my life. When I find something I want to do, I don't bang my head against the wall…I find someone already doing it. And I model success.

Now, I don't copy exactly. I start with what's working and make it my own. And I give credit where credit is due. I make a point of taking advice from people that have "earned the right" to give it. I want to learn from people who are doing what they are teaching.

Today in our education business, we bring current and aspiring real estate investors together to learn how to do more faster by collapsing time frames. Our thinking is that something that took us 10 years to master can be taught to others in 2. More sooner is better. And while most of our seminars are directly related to real estate investing and syndication (doing bigger deals by bringing together partners), our highest rated event by far is our annual goals retreat.

At the goals retreat, Create Your Future, I often joke that I've never had an original thought. Instead, I've learned from the masters and articulated a variety of ideas that help people create meaningful goals as well as the specific action plans necessary to ensure their achievement. I didn't invent goal setting. I refined it by standing on the shoulders of giants, then gave it my own style.

You can do the same thing. Anything you want to do with your life is possible. In fact, there is likely someone already doing it. So why not find out what they do and model that? Try it on for size. See if it works for you. Adjust as necessary. Ultimately, make it your own.

The best teachers, coaches, and mentors seek to be a catalyst—the proverbial pebble in the water—for their students to achieve greatness. Actor Jack Lemmon once said, "When you have done well in life, you have an obligation to send the elevator back down."

So, here's an excellent plan:

1. Seek out great teachers

2. Model success

3. Welcome great students and continue the process

The one thing that changed everything for me was realizing that the path had been forged already. All I had to do was find it and follow it. And do the work.

Look for evidence of success all around you. Then get going!

TWEETABLE
If it has been done, it can be done. And you can do it!

Robert Helms is a professional real estate investor with experience in nine states and six counties. As a former top producing real estate agent, Robert ranked in the top 1% of sales in the world's largest real estate organization. Robert's investment and development companies have projects valued at over $800 Million. He is the co-author of Equity Happens – Building Lifelong Wealth with Real Estate *and the host of the nationally syndicated radio show* The Real Estate Guys™, *now in its twenty-first year of broadcast. The podcast version of the show is one of the most downloaded podcasts on real estate and is heard in more than 190 countries.*

https://realestateguysradio.com

CHAPTER 11

The Art of the Bad Deal
by Sheldon Horowitz

"No."

"Please."

"I said the answer is NO!"

"Why not?"

"Because I said so."

At the tender age of two or three we are introduced to being on the short end of the stick of life. It's the first of many bad deals to come throughout our lifetime. Time and time again through our formative years we are beat over the head with that short end of the stick, yet we keep standing up and fighting back. That is the spirit of being a child in a nutshell. We instinctively know that "no" is simply meant to be used as a diving board to cannonball full force into the pool of opportunity and fun.

The bad deals keep on coming as we become adults. Our first job is with a boss that is dumb as rocks yet somehow is our boss and controls what we do at work. Then comes the realization that Mom and Dad don't have as much money saved for our college as we thought. Loans are available at 8.9% interest? You must be kidding me!

Into our working years, it seems the hits keep on coming. Our first paycheck shows up, and it is about 30% less than we were expecting. I didn't agree to all of this! What do you mean I have to pay the federal and state government from my hard-earned money? Social security, Medicare, insurance, and the list goes on. I need a vacation already!

Maybe this little story describes your first quarter century as though I have known you your whole life. Most likely you have experienced at least some of these things growing up. The simple answer to feeling differently about your experience is to be grateful and appreciate it for what it is. Eventually, the day will come when you are on the other side of the table, meaning you get to determine the terms of the deal. In other words, it will be your turn to make the rules and finally extract revenge for your lifetime of suffering.

The purpose of my story is to share one key philosophy that has drastically changed my life and the lives of many others who I have worked with over the years. I hope you are sitting down and holding on tight, as hearing this will completely rock your world. Throw everything you have learned right out the window. Here it is.

If something is worth 10, but you can get 12, ask for 9.

Huh?! Most people would say that you are cheating yourself or making a bad deal doing this.

"The Art of the Bad Deal"

For the past 10 years, I have been fortunate enough to be on the side of the table that has allowed me to be part of many lucrative partnerships. Deals have winners and losers and almost always have a net zero effect on the universe. Unlike deals, partnerships have the potential to change the world, forever. Taking less gives the other party a better chance at succeeding in your new partnership.

Successful partnerships have the characteristics of a tree. They are living organisms that need nurturing to get started, that occasionally need to be pruned, and that when cared for properly will create countless seeds that will, in time, create a forest.

First, you need to focus on developing the attitude of happily working for less. Once that is internalized, it is time to be open and ready to receive and recognize the opportunities that are coming your way.

Remember to nurture your partnership as though its life depends on it… because it does. An often overlooked aspect of creating successful partnerships is the commitment to improving yourself. The act of continual self-improvement carries with it many benefits, all of which help to greatly increase the value of your partnerships. Over the last decade, I have attended dozens of personal development seminars and absorbed upwards of ten thousand hours of lectures, speeches, and books on audio. At the beginning of my journey, my main purpose was to make more of myself to make more for myself. Experience has taught me that everyone is better served when I give more, and the best way to be able to give more is to become more.

The specifics of how this philosophy has changed my life are simple. It all stemmed from a thirty second conversation with Rick Roussin, the owner of the company that I work for.

At the end of a group meeting, he gave me a compliment regarding the speed with which I was growing within the company. With a twinkle in his eye, he followed it up with, "It would be amazing if you could help everyone in the company do the same."

That thirty seconds was less than one percent of an hour, and he probably forgot what he said minutes later. As far as I was concerned his words were covered in glue as they stuck in my mind to the point that I laid in bed at night working on making this become reality.

Less than two weeks later, I was in his office presenting the plan that would change everything. Eight years later, I was told I was going to be a vice president at our company, a goal which I had set almost four years prior.

I will close with a quote that has resonated with me since the first time I heard it and has been at the heart of some of my most important partnerships.

"It's amazing what you can accomplish when you don't care who gets the credit."
– Harry Truman

TWEETABLE
Everyone is better served when you give more. The best way to be able to give more is to become more.

Sheldon Horowitz is a Southern California native currently residing in Simi Valley. He has been happily married to Miranda Dawn since October 2015. Together they are raising their daughters Maliyah and Everley, ages 12 and 1 respectively. In 2014 he became a Ziglar Legacy Certified trainer to further his goal of positively impacting millions of people over his lifetime. Sheldon can be easily contacted thru his website www.sheldonhorowitz.net.

CHAPTER 12

How a Penniless Soldier Became a Business Leader

by Richard Haye

The radio crackled the familiar sound, and the unconscious focus honed in me over thousands of hours of training and combat operations took over. The voice on the call came in with carefully managed fear amidst the chaos unfolding in front of my fellow Soldiers. As I stood listening to the details, my heart rate began to climb and a strong sense of anxiety overcame me. I could do nothing to help them from here. It was too late.

The vehicle call sign came in. I knew it well from my early days in first platoon. The details of the damages and situation were all I needed to hear to know, on this day, many lives would never be the same. My mentor was gone. Friendships forged since my first day in the unit ended in an instant; the conclusion being the ultimate sacrifice any Soldier can make. As I continued to listen, the scene being described was grizzly and filled with devastation beyond anything we had yet to experience in two tours in Iraq. The vehicle had been hit by a particularly devastating explosive compound our own special forces taught the Iraqi military years prior. The back half of the Stryker had its roof peeled open by the blast. Bench seats were over a hundred meters away. Perhaps worst of all was the several thousand-pound engine blown on top of the driver, pinning him into the burning wreckage, making a rescue an impossible task.

My mind took over, running through battle drills and what I might be doing if only I could be there to help; though this was yet another impossible task. I reminded myself of the failure I was to my friends as I was physically unable to go on missions. My breathing slowed as I struggled to shift my mind back to the call. There I stood, controlled by my mind, betrayed by my body...The adrenaline surging through me gave me a brief reprieve from the sharp continuous pain I had been enduring for months on end, but soon the adrenaline faded and the pain came back, reminding me of everything I couldn't do.

My thoughts shifted to my mentor and the beginning of my friendship with him. One of my first days in the unit, Staff Sergeant Santos took some time to get to know me even though I was not one of his Soldiers. He spoke of his time as a Private and advice he was given. "Evaluate every interaction you have, hear about, and see as you go through life. Imagine two buckets, one for things you see that you like and want to use, and the other for everything you think are not good habits or ways to interact with others. When you approach life this way and fill your buckets, you can never go wrong." This simple concept has taken me through some of the greatest challenges in life and has shaped me greatly.

The last conversation I had with Staff Sergeant Santos was a few hours earlier, just before he set out on the last mission he would lead his squad on. "Hey, Hey, Hey, Baby I got your money, don't you worry," he sang as he walked up to the motor pool guard shack. Part of his routine before missions was to stop by and see how I was holding up; he knew I was having a difficult time handling not being able to go on missions due to a back injury I would, years later, undergo spinal fusion to repair. We made casual small talk as usual, and he left me with a daily dose of sanity as he reminded me I had "given everything my body could handle and there was no shame in it."

Moments later my friend, Specialist Mowl, approached me with his usual cheerful yet quiet confidence and sharp intellect. Our conversations always had some sort of high-level concept layered throughout, and this day's was no different. We had worked together on various occasions, though we were in separate platoons. He was one of the most intelligent men I have ever known. Months before deployment we were both placed into an Arabic language course for our respective platoons. Throughout the course I was able to get to know him on a deeper level and learned he hoped to go work at the defense language institute after his time in Iraq was up. I had done well in the course; Mowl on the other hand was brilliant and learned Arabic faster than I thought possible. Even so, he never bragged as he believed in a healthy helping of humility. The conversation this morning took a turn for light-hearted topics and guilty pleasures conjured up as a result of extensive stress during deployments. At the time I didn't think much of what he said before walking to his Stryker for the last time. "If I never had to shave again I could die happy," he said with a grin.

The weight of these words echoing through my mind crushed me as I learned his face had been badly injured in the blast. He survived seven months of intensive treatments and life support before he succumbed to his injuries. The cruel irony did not escape me in this moment. After this day he would never shave again, and I truly hope it is a sign he was able to die happy. Thoughts about my purpose in life plagued me. Was I doing what I was meant to do? Did I take all the good in my life for granted? How could I ever live a life filled with enough purpose to justify their sacrifice?

The answers never came to me as long and as hard as I thought about it. In this moment, I decided to live the best life I could, to continually strive to be better than the day before, and to dedicate myself to helping others achieve success and live their dreams; only then would I be honoring their sacrifice to protect the freedom and dreams of our people. I would never do anything I didn't want to do again, and I would cast away the worry about that which I could not control.

Deciding to never do anything you don't want to do is not an easy path. I was facing an extended period before I would be back in the states; and my unit was under incredible pressure every moment of the day to execute missions shorthanded because of the losses. My unending desire to help my friends would never come to be, as I was not able to go on missions again. This presented new, unforeseen challenges. Many of my fellows resented me as they continued the grind day after day; longtime friends stopped talking to me one by one. Before long I felt completely alone, controlled by my mind, betrayed by my body…. As we continued to lose people, continued sending Soldiers away on medivacs, the emotional stress piled on. Nearly an entire platoon was unable to go on missions, yet I was alone. Being alone turned to verbal beat downs from people I once considered close to me. I began to doubt everything I did, every thought I had. Every breath I took led to a question. *Am I living the best life the best way I can? Am I worthless and lying to myself?*

When we returned, I was moved to a staff position where I waited until my eventual transfer to the warrior transition unit to undergo the medical board process. My days transformed from contributing to the readiness of a hardened infantry unit to sitting in doctor's office waiting rooms and case manager appointments. My childhood dream was to serve in the infantry until retirement. What was I to do now? My skills consisted of "point and shoot," and "close with and destroy:" training men how to fight and survive in a world beyond our world, a world filled with unknown enemies who do not follow the rules. Life took me from one place to another, a room at my sister's in Kansas City, to a high-rise overlooking Sun Devil Stadium in sunny Tempe, Arizona.

Back in Missouri I lived paycheck to paycheck with short stops at unfulfilling jobs, trying to adjust to a world I no longer understood. Eventually, I found a job with the railroad and stumbled upon something that took me back to the moment that changed it all; I found a profession dedicated to a methodology of continued improvement and helping others learn and grow: Lean Six Sigma. Lean Six Sigma is created entirely to make help us do three things: improve the way we work, increase efficiency and effectiveness in everything we do, and transform the behaviors and culture of organizations. I found myself studying all I could find about it every moment I had free; hundreds of hours were poured in to learning its ins and outs. I began to reach out to as many professionals in the field as I could find to learn about their experiences, their journeys, and how to be successful by sharing my knowledge with others. What I learned was not easy to hear. I had no experience in the field of continuous improvement and operational excellence and no college degree. "No one gets hired in this without it," I was told. My struggles continued and I was running out of options. If I was to succeed I would have to reimagine my path to success. I researched company after company associated with this methodology until finally I found one where I could get a foot in the door.

I was letting caution to the wind by taking a chance with an entry-level position at a company which utilized Lean Six Sigma. The time had come to prove everyone wrong. Finally, I had the break I was looking for. Was this the answer to living and doing only the things I wanted to do? I was working the night shift and quite a bit of overtime on the weekends while my days were often spent with my kids and putting in time doing additional studying and school. I began sharing my knowledge, volunteering for any opportunity to do more for the team, and helping to improve the way we worked. I continued my networking efforts, and before long I networked to the top of my company. The next thing I knew, I was leading teams on high impact projects resulting in massive financial gains, coaching leaders of a top 50 company on the Fortune 500 list and indirectly saving lives with improved business results on a lifesaving product.

The last 15 years of my life have evolved from training and coaching young Soldiers, to training business leaders, small business owners, home business professionals, and network marketers (why should I use my skills only to make money for the corporations). The years of hard work, striving to improve every day, and helping others has come full circle. "What I want to do" has not always translated to lounging and relaxing for hours on end. Devotion to my skills, expanding my knowledge capital, and working at every element of my life has tallied thousands of hours of work, but is it really work if it is what you want to do? Today I still work to help save lives, but in a way, it is my life that's been saved. The ability to help others reach their dreams of time and financial freedom and show them that it is indeed possible to live a life of "only what I want to do," has been worth every second I have dedicated to helping lift others up around me.

My one thing that changed it all was a moment in time filled with pain and a sacrifice impossible to repay in a thousand lifetimes. But in this life, I am living the best way I know how... for others, "because it's what I want to do."

TWEETABLE

Is life happening to you or are you deciding? Everything is a decision. The only way to get where you want to go is by making that choice.

Richard Haye is a speaker, coach, and trainer in company growth and efficiency. He speaks to small and large groups including Fortune 20 companies. He served six years in the army infantry with the 2nd Infantry Division as a part of the Army's first Stryker Brigade and two tours in Iraq. To contact Richard about business coaching: Richard.haye3@hotmail.com

CHAPTER 13

You Are Not Forgotten

The Afghanistan Memory Wall

by Ron White

I served in the United States Navy from 2002-2010 and was deployed to Afghanistan in 2007. I was an Intelligence Specialist. IS1, Petty Officer 1st class.

I'm not a combat veteran. I did 51 convoys, but I saw no combat action. There is nothing extraordinary about my service or deployment. It was just a regular deployment like many others. But countless men and women were in extraordinary circumstances. Combat veterans and too many others paid the ultimate sacrifice. I help tell the story of these sacrifices in a unique way.

Maybe the best place to start is where my mindset was in 2011. I was 38 years old and very discouraged.

A significant relationship with my girlfriend had ended badly. I had been out of the military for one year, and I missed that camaraderie and sense of purpose. My business was stagnating and I was searching for something.

I had just been dethroned as the two time national memory champion. I was like, "Man, what's next? Are my teeth going to fall out?"

It was a time of mental turmoil and depression for me. I gained weight, drank, and slept a lot. I was in a mammoth-sized rut.

One night at the bar while watching the ice float in my vodka, I reflected on a question a friend had asked me a few years earlier. She asked, "How long would it take you to memorize the Vietnam Wall?"

She knew my patriotism, my love for country, my military background, and that I'm a memory expert, so it wasn't an odd question. I gave my answer that day, and the conversation moved on to other things.

Years later, sitting at the bar mesmerized by my vodka, I pondered that question again. It was like a bolt of lightning hit me. My back straightened, my head lifted, and my eyes focused up and forward. I set the glass down.

A smirk began to grow across my face. It was the answer. It was the answer to everything. In an instant, I had a purpose again. I had a mission.

Many times in my life the right idea came into my mind and I didn't recognize it. Many times I acted too slowly and missed the chance. Many times I didn't fight for it.

This time, for once in my life, I saw this idea for what it was. It was my one thing that changed everything.

I grabbed onto the idea like the lifeline to me it was. I began searching everywhere online. I was Googling terms like "United States Military deaths in Afghanistan."

After an hour or so of searching, I found a total I believed was accurate: 1,853.

1,853 US military members paid the ultimate sacrifice in Afghanistan as of December 2011.

I leaned back in my chair and the wheels in my mind began to turn. The wheels that had been slowed the last 12 months with depression, unhealthy food, and alcohol were feverishly working on math problems.

I grabbed some wrinkled paper on my desk and began to scribble calculations.

"55.59 days... that's not even two months. I could do it in two months and then take an extra month just to be safe. Three months. I can do this."

And so it began. So what was the project? My purpose?

It was a vision.

As a nation we say, "You are not forgotten." I know we mean it, but I think we mean it as a group. I wanted to say individually to every single person who gave their life that they were not forgotten.

Not to get spooky or anything, but it was my *Field of Dreams* moment. You know, the movie where the guy hears a voice to build a baseball diamond in a cornfield. The voice said, "If you build it they will come."

It was almost the exact same thing for me.

But I didn't know if they would come. I didn't know if anyone would care, but the desire had been lit, and I was certain I had to do it.

My vision was me standing at a wall or a board. I was writing out the names of everyone who died in Afghanistan from memory.

Imagine you are watching the Vietnam Wall being written out by hand by one person and imagine that person was doing it 100% from memory. That was the idea, but for Afghanistan.

A simple idea but a massive project.

I had calculated that it would take me two months to memorize the 1,853 heroes' names. But that was an overly optimistic and grossly wrong calculation. It ended up taking 10 months.

It was less of a feat of memory as it was a feat of discipline.

Over the next 10 months, everywhere I went I had a black binder with the names printed out, 1,853 of them.

You'd find me on a train in Europe or at a baseball game in Texas with my black binder out memorizing. It was a year spent in extreme solitude.

When I began the process, I didn't know any of them personally. Now I feel like I know all of them. Not just their names, I feel like I know them.

You may find it hard to believe that as driven as I was, as sure as I was of what I was doing, I only told a few close friends what I was doing during that 10 months of memorizing. My high school friend Brian, Kyle Wilson, a friend and my mental coach for my USA Memory Championship wins, and a former US Navy SEAL TC Cummings were my confidants.

I remember vividly three months into this process talking with TC. He said, "Ronnie, I don't think you see the full scope of this project. I don't think you understand fully what it's going to be like."

He said that family members would stand there in anticipation of me writing their loved one's name. He said they would wait for hours and as I got close to the name, they would begin to get teary-eyed and say, "Oh, he's about to write the name."

I smiled and just thanked him for being such a good friend. I felt he was exaggerating the response the wall would get.

However, he described exactly and almost prophetically what happens every single time I write the wall.

In the *Field of Dreams* movie, there is a scene where James Earl Jones' character Terence is talking to Kevin Costner's character Ray. He says,

"People will come, Ray...for reasons they can't even fathom...as innocent as children, longing for the past...for it is money they have and peace they lack...The memories will be so thick they'll have to brush them away from their faces."

Although these are lines from a movie, this tells the story of what happens at the Afghanistan Memory Wall every time.

TC saw what James Earl Jones' character saw. He was seeing the emotional connection people were going to have with this. I didn't see it, but I knew I was drawn to it. I knew I had to do it.

Now, every time I set up the wall, I brief my helpers beforehand because I know what is coming and they never do.

I say, "I don't know when it will happen today, but it will. Someone is going to walk by this wall and ask what it is. In an instant their eyes are going to fill with tears and they will be barely able to contain themselves. Then they will give us a name and ask us if it's on the wall. I will take them to that name and they will stand in silence with tears running down their face."

Every time it is my *Field of Dreams* moment.

February 28, 2013 I set the wall up for the first time in public. By 7:30am I was writing.

My mom, dad, helpers, a few friends including Kyle Wilson, and the news media were there, but no one else.

Would anyone come?

Would anyone care?

I didn't know. But I knew I had to write. This was the moment.

As I wrote that day, the radio stations began talking about it. TV news crews began to broadcast it. The city was waking up to the memorial taking place, and I had no idea what was going on as I wrote.

A grandmother who lost her grandson in Afghanistan turned her car around and headed to see the wall. On her way, she began calling the other gold star families she knew. They headed to the wall like nails to a magnet.

A man in a Harley Davidson jacket got the call and climbed on his motorcycle and hurried to the wall to see his son's name.

A manager in a building nearby heard about the wall and arrived at it in tears. He pointed to Lance Corporal Cody Childers and said, "He was a Lieutenant."

I said, "No I think he was a Lance Corporal."

He once again said in a low tone, "He was a Lieutenant."

I replied, "Are you sure? I think he was a Lance Corporal."

Then his voice became stern and clear, and for the first time, I saw his eyes. They were bloodshot, and he pointed to his chest and said, "NO. I was his Lieutenant." In an instant, I knew the gravity of the situation. Cody was one of his men. He deserved a rank he would never get. I said nothing, and he said, "I'm going to call his mom" and walked away.

Soon there was a crowd of 100 or more people finding names and paying their respects. I couldn't believe it.

TC was right.

A grandmother waited four hours for me to write her grandson's name. She called her daughter so they could watch me write the name "PFC Austin Staggs." After the long wait, as I got near Austin on the wall, I turned and said, "I will be writing Austin's name soon."

They gathered behind me and I wrote "Sgt Barry..." and before I could write his last name they said, "That's Barry."

Then I wrote "Private..." and they said, "That's Devin." To me it had always been Private Devin Harris and Sergeant Barry Jarvis. To them it was Barry and Devin.

The wall was becoming personal for me. These men must have died with the son and grandson of these women right here beside me. And I had no idea. I wrote PFC Austin Staggs, and as I did, my hand trembled. I then turned, and Austin's family and I shared an embrace.

If this was the *Field of Dreams* movie, they would be walking out of a cornfield right now. As darkness crept over the horizon, a man approached my cousin and asked, "What are you going to do if it gets dark and he isn't done?"

My cousin replied, "We hadn't thought of that."

I was not aware of this conversation because I was writing, but my cousin said the man left and within 30 minutes was back with industrial-size lights, the kind you see on the highway when they are doing construction in the middle of the night.

Whoever he was, he had connections, and he was moved closer to the wall so he could do his part.

The city was coming out for this.

They were coming out of the cornfield to honor the fallen.

It was one of the most magical days of my life.

I have spent the last five years of my life repeating this day over and over, taking the wall around the United States to honor our heroes. Today the wall holds 2,300+ heroes and is still growing although a lot more slowly now. It is nearly 7,000 words and takes 10 hours to write out.

For me, this memorial is the one thing that changed everything. Honoring and giving respect to others has given me purpose and a mission which I would not trade.

TWEETABLE
Honoring and giving respect to others has given me purpose and a mission which I would not trade.

Ron White is a veteran of the United States Navy who served in Afghanistan in 2007. He is also a two-time USA Memory Champion who held the USA record for the fastest to memorize a deck of cards for two years. He travels the United States with a 52-foot long wall where he writes out the names of the fallen from the war in Afghanistan from memory to honor them and to say you are not forgotten. To listen to the podcast that tells these amazing stories, please visit www.americasmemory.com

CHAPTER 14

Life is Never "Either, Or"

by Eric Tait, MD

'Hold on, hold on, he was found face down where?" That was the only response I could muster as my mother tried to explain that her oldest brother was on a mechanical ventilator in a hospital, the very same hospital where he was a staff member and practicing physician.

I was a college junior at the same school my uncle had attended on his way to medical school, and my 20-year-old brain didn't know how to process this situation.

My uncle was my mentor. I was following in his footsteps in many ways. Although we were not especially close, he always fueled my dreams of becoming a doctor.

He was a third-generation physician and a large figure in the community. The expectation that he would carry on the "family business" was high, and I wondered if that expectation in some way had led him to his current hospital bed.

Even at a young age I had an entrepreneurial spirit. I started working outside the home at age nine, not because I had to but because I wanted to. From shoveling snow for neighbors, to working as a handyman at an art gallery, to maintenance work in commercial buildings, I was always looking for ways to become financially independent.

But talk to anyone who knew me growing up, and they can tell you that they knew I would be a doctor.

Like many children, I received the Fisher Price doctor kit as a Christmas present. The difference for me was that I was expected to be the fourth generation in our family to practice medicine.

Some might say it was an indoctrination process on the part of my family, and that may have been the case. Children emulate what they see, and I had a prominent uncle who was a surgeon with a thriving medical practice. It was easy to envision myself doing the same. But my entrepreneurial streak remained undaunted.

To this day, I remember my father admonishing me to "live up to your full potential," because although I was top student and athlete in grade school and high school, he knew that I coasted by on natural talent and ability. You see, my father is an immigrant, and a stereotypically hard working one at that. He's also the prototypical Renaissance man. Although he was an executive at a major television network when I was growing up, he also explored diverse areas of interest. He wrote plays, composed music, sketched, and painted portraits. He had (and still has) an amazing intellectual curiosity and always encouraged me to explore everything that interested me.

With my father's artistic undertakings and my mother's pride in her family's line of physicians, my immediate family set up an interesting dichotomy for me. I could follow the path to medicine that had been laid before me or I could follow my non-medical passions. I thought, why not do both?

Well, medicine is a jealous mistress, and the time commitment and dedication to becoming a physician and then practicing medicine are often all-consuming. At least that's how most doctors live their lives in medicine. But even in college, I began to have doubts about that "either, or" model of life.

I was able to drive down from college with my mother to visit my uncle in the hospital. Seeing him attached to machines and not consciously aware of our presence was jarring. This man, a pillar in the medical community, was now a patient in his own hospital. During his illness I came to understand that his life as a physician was not all what it seemed.

We all have family traditions and legends that guide our understanding of who we are and our place in the world. In our family we all believed my uncle reveled in his career as "doctor." He was well respected and had all the trappings of financial success—he owned nice cars, lived in a beautiful home, and sent my cousins to private school. But there was more to the story. The truth was his second wife had "nudged" him into medicine, possibly against his natural inclinations, and now I wonder if that "nudge" played a part in his current condition.

I began to think back to my interactions with him as an adult, and one episode that happened less than a year before his hospitalization came to mind. It was the occasion of my grandmother's death. Most of our family came back to town for the funeral, including my mother, her two brothers and their cousin. There they were, sitting and reminiscing about their mother and aunt. Libations were flowing and everyone was happy.

My uncle, the surgeon, was leading a discussion around taxes and investing in a way that I found fascinating. At the end of it, my mother made a comment to me in passing that my uncle "really should have gone into business." At the time, I found the comment very strange. Because he was carrying forward the family name in the medical field, I assumed he was doing what he loved. The truth, we would soon learn, was very different,

Although my uncle was still a physician, he no longer had a thriving medical practice. In fact, it appeared that once his second wife died, he had descended into an apathetic malaise around medicine that none of us were fully aware of.

Now, as he was fighting for his life in an intensive care unit, we were left to figure out what was really going on in his life.

I can't fully describe what it's like to have what I believed to be the truth unravel before my eyes. It was hard to process, especially as I was following in his footsteps.

This was not some lightning strike moment or epiphany, but a gradual awakening to the fact that all was not as it seemed. I was already in the process of applying to medical schools and a few were high on my list. Yet, I still had the pull of entrepreneurship in my soul.

Once in college, I gave up my physical labor jobs, and instead, my roommate and I started a barbershop and sandwich business out of our freshman dorm, supplying hungry students when the cafeteria was closed. This thriving business piqued my interest in pursuing a combined MD/MBA (Masters of Business Administration) programs.

Back in the hospital, as we met with doctors and surgeons caring for my uncle, they gave us a bleak prognosis. He'd had a massive heart attack and his brain had been deprived of oxygen for an unknown amount of time. His heart was very weak and none of the local surgeons wanted to take the risk of operating on their colleague lest he die at their hands on the operating table. But there was a new surgeon in town. He had just come from Houston, Texas where he had trained and worked at Baylor College of Medicine.

He gave it to us straight. He would need to do a very difficult bypass surgery to try and create new blood flow to my uncle's heart. He told us that there was a good chance that he would not be able to restart his heart after the procedure because it had been so badly damaged, but he was willing to give it a try.

It just so happened Baylor College of Medicine was on my list of medical schools because they were establishing a dual degree MD/MBA program. At the time, I didn't realize the serendipity of the situation, and I can't say I made a conscious decision to attend Baylor because of my uncle's health situation. But I don't believe in coincidences either.

I left for Baylor a year and a half later to pursue a dual degree program in medicine and business, determined to become the best doctor that I could be as well as to become financially independent as fast as I could so that I had the freedom to pursue all the projects and passions that I desired.

It did not disappoint! Spending the next few years in pursuit of both medical and business degree was exhilarating. It was a crush of information, but I had never felt more alive. I was in pursuit of the two things that I wanted and had no doubts that I was on the right path.

A few years later our extended family had the chance to be together again, this time for a joyous occasion. My sister was getting married, and we all traveled to Bermuda for the ceremony. It was the first international trip for my uncle since his successful bypass surgery. He was tenuous physically and had some lasting mental deficits from the time his brain was deprived of oxygen, but he was in good spirits. I was able to spend time with him and tell him all about my dual degree program. He seemed genuinely proud that I was on the way to achieving my goals and he had a great time on the trip. So much so that he overindulged a bit and ended up in heart failure during the wedding reception. Still a medical student, I was the one who diagnosed his condition and rode with him in the ambulance to the hospital.

My uncle lived a few more years in this condition, and he made sure that both of his daughters finished college and launched successfully into their careers. But I wonder to this day what his life would have looked like had he decided to explore his true passions.

When I started medical school I wanted to become a surgeon like my uncle. But as I experienced my different clinical rotations, I gravitated towards primary care. I liked the idea of creating long-lasting relationships with people to help them overcome, or at least manage, their medical conditions. I came to realize that in many cases, chronic medical illnesses were borne of stressful lives and unfulfilled dreams. Unhealthy lifestyles often stemmed from an unhealthy outlook and unhealthy circumstances. If I wanted to change health at the root cause level, it required looking beyond the disease presentation. It required an examination of the person's circumstances and choices. What I found was, more often than not, people had unfulfilled lives and were living for the expectations of others. This suppression of one's true calling can lead to stress, latent depression, or other psychological issues which lead to unhealthy habits.

I ultimately decided to pursue a career in internal medicine and joined an existing medical group after my training. At the same time, I started investing heavily to realize my dream of financial independence. It was so much a part of who I was that when I took my original job, I made sure that I only ever worked a four-day workweek so that I had time to pursue my business interests. I was willing to take less money at the outset of my career to build a life that supported who I was and who I wanted to be.

After a few years of successful investing, something completely unexpected happened. Physician colleagues saw what I was doing and wanted to join in. The last 10 years have brought massive upheaval and uncertainty to the medical profession, and physicians are feeling nervous about the future. In the past, if medicine was not necessarily your passion, one could often grin and bear it because of the high compensation and personal autonomy that medicine allowed, but those days are ending.

Over 50% of physicians are objectively suffering from burnout and are actively looking to leave the profession. Similar to my patients, if you look at the root cause, the combination of long hours, decreasing autonomy, and decreasing payment is destroying doctors' passion for the profession. Fortunately, I've never personally felt that way, and I'm convinced it's because I was able to construct a well-balanced life that affords me time to pursue myriad passions.

After hearing from other physicians, we decided to expand our firm to help them create a more fulfilling life in medicine. By creating a clear road, physicians can get a glimpse of a future where they control their own personal destiny, and they will realize they don't have to sacrifice their whole existence to "one thing."

That realization does wonders for their personal outlook and attitude towards medicine going forward. And for me, it continues to fuel my passion to help others live the life they want to live without worrying about how the outside world views their choices.

There is no feeling like telling another human being that life does not have to be "either, or" and seeing them have that "aha" moment when it sinks in. Through imagination, planning, and following your heart, your life can be "and, both" as well.

TWEETABLE
We should never give up who we are in pursuit of what we do, even as doctors. We must live life whole or risk losing it all.

Eric S. Tait MD, MBA helps physicians create lives of meaning. His firm The Physician's Road shows clients how to achieve financial independence, freeing their time to pursue fulfilling professional lives, create deeper relationships, and achieve better health. Eric writes and speaks for audiences nationally and internationally on money, investing, and creating a life that integrates work and family.

Contact him at Eric@thephysiciansroad.com

CHAPTER 15

More Than Expected
How My "Impossible" Pregnancy Shattered My Misconceptions

by Lynn Bodnar

The light is so bright, piercing into my eyes. I can't really see, squinting to comprehend what is going on. Another searing wave of pain crashes over me. *This will be over soon, right? I can handle it, right?* I look to my left, see my husband there and it gives me strength. As they tie down my arms onto boards straight out to my sides, I feel the panic of being constrained. *Is this really necessary?* I've actually done this before, but it's just so different this time. Because it's an emergency situation, everyone was so focused and efficient. No time for questions or distractions from the matter at hand.

As the nerve block travels down my spine, it does its job well. Within several minutes I feel nothing. Just Breathe. The team is so busy, in the zone, right where I need them to be. Relieved of the unbearable pain, I zone out and wonder... *How did I get here? Is this actually happening?*

As it turns out, vasectomies do "grow back." After we had our third child, we decided our family picture looked complete. Five faces filled the frame. My husband dutifully had his vasectomy shortly after our third child. I know this for sure, because I was there, I watched it. It was fascinating, the doctor enjoyed showing me a step-by-step tutorial on how performing a vasectomy works. He even lifted up little noodley things, talking about not to forget "these guys," or that makes for trouble.

Did my husband go back for *all* of his scheduled "swimmers" checks? Yes. Even at the one year mark. So, we thought we were in the clear, home free!

Five and a half years passed. Thoughts of conception were a distant dot in my rearview mirror. Besides, I was in my 43rd year of life, way too old. My youngest was in kindergarten and soon heading for first grade! I had been a stay-at-home-mom for over 12 years at this point. Did I dare start making new goals for...ME? New career thoughts? What were my options? Couldn't go back where I left off 12 years ago. Either way, the year 2007 began with the exciting thought process of reinventing myself.

Don't get me wrong. I was grateful to have been a stay-at-home mom. I loved every minute (or nearly every minute). Fully diving into the job, I learned about parenting and how to grow these little darlings. With no training, like all parents, I created my own. I read all the books. I debated all the debates—breastfeed or formula, Ferberize or sleeping with us, "Is another language crucial at three years old?" Even seriously sleep deprived (my kryptonite), I noticed they were somehow surviving, one could argue, even thriving.

However, the stealth parental programming had started and I was quickly infused with what's expected. Our society dictates how it's done, how your kids need to properly grow up and show up. I felt total pressure that my kids go down the "right" path, that I was supposed to know everything to do and be sure to get it right. Like, no piano lessons? Clearly that kid's brain will not develop, and forget any hopes of advanced math. College could be out. Doesn't matter that the kid was still in preschool.

The clues could be subtle or overt. Early and often, parents are pelted with judgment. Like, oftentimes, in preschool, kids create an "All About Me" poster and present it in class. Naturally, I helped them choose some of their favorite things and peppered it with family info: books, treats, movies, siblings, pets, etc. I guided my child with their project, they put together the masterpiece, and we showed up on the due date. My jaw dropped as I saw the others kids' presentations. These three and four-year-old kids were amazing! Looking at "our" poster, with the half-eaten gummy bear hanging off (I mean, after all, it's their favorite treat and there was an entire car ride to school), stickers randomly scattered in a way that made sense to my child with dog hair sticking to it, I quickly learned I missed the message. I was supposed to make it look amazing, not my kid. They would have their turn to make their own "All About Me" poster another day. I was clearly clueless.

Like a frog in hot water, I slowly got sucked into the culturally dictated acceptable terms of how to make choices and how to parent. The comparisons and judgments were smothering, and I was fully immersed and unaware. My "mombie" hat of conformity was affixed to my head and I didn't even stop to think. I was just too tired. Like everyone, I wanted to be a great parent. And fit in. Trying to keep up with the "shoulds" and the fear of screwing each kid up irreparably, I just kept my nose to the grindstone of compliance.

That's what you do. That's what THEY say. "It's in the kids' best interests." Among the "good mom" requirements are:

Be sure you regularly volunteer at school because it's your job to see the school is doing its job, ensure your kid is front and center and, oh yeah, make the world a better place.

Be sure you can explain your choices and others agree with you. You conform.

Be sure you prove you are doing something, are contributing, are valid, not just staying home, lacking ambition with a face stuffed with bon bons. OR you show up when you are not at work to prove you are involved in your kid's life.

Be sure you show up with the perfect cupcake. On time. Every time. Properly themed. With appropriate contingencies for all possible culinary conflicts.

I hadn't recognized my cycle of "stuck." I was blessed with my children and the mom-gig, and I was ready and excited for the next stages. Under the surface, I didn't realize how much I was trying to shake off being judged while knowing I was oh-so-imperfect.

Since we were done having children, I had some girl surgery. As I was heading for my post-op checkup, I felt kind of weird. I had these nagging recognizable symptoms but...nah, it would be impossible.

Awkwardly, I talked with my surgeon about being late, blaming the surgery for affecting my normal, consistent periods. He ominously mentioned that if I were pregnant, to be sure to have a C-section or there would be serious implications.

As I drove over an hour home, my rational brain was reviewing my symptoms: sore tatas, frequenting the bathroom, mega tired, nausea, and the kicker, a sinus infection. I always would get one in the first trimester of my pregnancies. So I pulled over to the Target by my home. At the pharmacy, I purchased the cheapest pregnancy test. I followed the directions like a pro ('cause I am). Two blue lines appeared. *Seriously?* I bought the cheap test and got a false reading!

That afternoon I had an appointment with my regular doctor for the sinus infection. She prescribed antibiotics. As an afterthought, I casually said, "Oh, strangely enough, I had this weird, false, positive pregnancy test from a defective tester, and, like isn't that just stupid and impossible.... haha." She insisted we check. After waiting what seemed like three hours, she bounded into the room and excitedly announced it's "very positive." Shock, denial, freakout, speech-lessness, and free falling. Maybe the doc didn't understand THIS IS IMPOSSIBLE. VA- SEC-TO-MY. CANNOT HAVE A BABY. Been that way for several years. Keep up with me here.

Turns out, it might not have been the doctor who wasn't comprehending.

How am I going to handle this? How is my body going to get through this? What do I do now? With the very small voice, getting smaller, what about me?

First, to tell my husband. I went home, decided to get a sitter, and took him out to dinner. We would need to have uninterrupted mommy and daddy time. We pulled up into the restaurant parking lot, and I wished I had a cute, clever way of delivering the news. I was more like a chipmunk on speed rambling incoherently but not actually saying anything. He patiently asked me to take a breath, and just tell him what was up, that I was kind of scaring him that something was seriously wrong. Deep breath taken, I looked at him and said, "It looks like we are going to have a baby. I am pregnant." His hands still on the steering wheel, he stared off into space for a few seconds. Then said, "Wow! How did we get so lucky to be having another child? We are so blessed, we must be good parents! This is incredible!" I couldn't have dreamed of a better reaction. My mind was swirling with denial and fear of starting all over again, but he cut right to the chase: the big picture. And he was right, it would be a blessing. Only I was terrified.

That would be the best reaction ever. I would find some supportive and kind folks, but, alas, there were plenty of obnoxious, unhelpful, thoughtless and hurtful comments.

Most common was an insincere, "Oh, that's great news. We're so happy for you, right, honey?" with a sharp elbow to his ribs, "Go get checked—now!"

There was the "Congrats! But if that were me I'd kill myself." Nice. I'm glad I wasn't struggling or that would be really hard to hear.

"Better you than me." Apparently so.

Many thought I was completely confused about how babies were made. "Wow, Lynn, haven't you figured out how this works yet? Haven't you heard of birth control? Why would you risk this at your age?" Ouch.

Even more fun was the frequent implication that I must have had an affair. One "lovely" lady, in front of my kids, loudly proclaimed it had to be an affair! After prattling on and on, she concludes, "I mean, that just doesn't happen!" Interesting to notice how easily that explanation occurred to her.

There were also beautiful people who simply showed kindness. Friends who genuinely got excited and even said "We are having a baby!" My sister-in-law literally almost jumped through the roof. They were a handful of people who didn't bring judgment and myopic comments, but instead gave a sense of support when I most needed it. I was so grateful, as I was struggling between gratitude and the guilt I felt of stuckness, selfishness and worry.

The baby arrives in the world, via C-section. A date had been planned but she surprises us and comes early. Makes sense.

As we reframed our new family picture to include six faces, I started to feel like I was watching the same movie over again. Like rewatching a movie, I saw things I never noticed before. I started to question, why do I do the things I do? Why do I just follow the "right way" of doing things? Had I ever questioned the ingrained expectations? I slowly realized my life had become on autopilot.

I remembered back to the decision to be a stay-at-home mom, and how I was convinced I would never lose myself. I had to squarely face that, for years now, I had been growing others but not growing myself.

I started to awaken. I started to rethink everything. I went through a process. Examined my beliefs. I committed to personal development, opened to new experiences, and often asked "Who says?" My eyes opened to my illusions. I was amazed what I found when I took my head out of the sand and looked around.

This experience delivered numerous key a-ha's that transformed my life. Here are several:

- Things grow back! The "impossible" in my mind actually became the reality. I learned how to be gentle with myself instead of freaking out.

- People often react entirely from where they are coming from without consideration to how you are feeling, what you are thinking or possibly panicking about. Being more aware, really listening and asking questions from kindness is what I strive for.

- The world will continue to spin on its axis if I take care of my needs. Learning true self-care has been a game changer, measurably increasing my happiness, attitude, and outlook.

- I sadly felt I needed to prove my worth and validity by doing a great mom-job (doing everything), because it seemed, without a W2, I was not as valued or respected. I awakened to knowing that being a great mom is how I define it, and making heart-centered decisions was proof enough, for me and my family.

- I used to worry about what people thought of me, now I focus on what I think of me.

- You can't find yourself if you are not looking. I had to open up to take a true and honest look at myself. I found that my happiness and fulfillment were waiting for me.

- Moms (parents) need each other more than ever. We are all different and do things differently. It's long overdue to replace judgment and criticism with support, understanding, and kindness. We are in this together. Criticism is uncool and only debilitates the critic.

- We are handed scripts by our culture, and it's very difficult to rewrite these roles and expectations. It takes the willingness to face some of our biggest fears—looking stupid, "not doing it right," not belonging, and failing our children—to be able to change.

The more I opened to my truth, the more I realized that moms, dads, and all of us benefit from a fresh, illusion shifting look at what we truly believe, what we do and why we do it. Creating our own intentional expectations brings Having a bonus, unexpected, "impossible" baby at 43 years old? It's the one thing that changed everything. It gifted me a reframe to my life that had stagnated on autopilot and fear. Joyously, gratefully, incredibly, and absolutely no give-backs!

TWEETABLE
I used to worry about what others thought of me now I just try to focus on what I think of me.

After 10 years with a Fortune 100 company, Lynn Bodnar closed up her briefcase to be a professional mom where she would have (no) control of her day and master the art of volunteering. Her family most admires her fearlessness in the face of rejection, like making meals no one eats. Grateful to be living an intentional life traveling, learning, laughing, growing, and helping others journey through shifting their illusions, Lynn invites you to experience the full- length "TMI" story, no labor on your part. Questions? Can relate? Want to share? For the full story and more, visit lynnbodnar.com or Facebook: Lynn Bodnar, Author

CHAPTER 16

From Zero to $70 Million
Doing Syndication Differently
by Dave Zook

M y not-so-secret secret is that I have raised over $70 million in real estate ventures and in the ATM space just in the last several years partnering with investors in multiple successful transactions.

Early on in my adult life and until my mid-30s, I had no interest in real estate. My dad was a real estate investor such that he parked his extra capital from his very successful business in real estate and he self-managed some of his own residential rentals which actually ended up working well for him, but it came with its own set of issues.

I did not want anything to do with that, and I knew there had to be a better way to make money, so I pursued business. I started several businesses, I partnered with others and I started to have lots of success.

I did some small real estate deals, but I wasn't focused on it at all. After several years of building my businesses and eventually getting into a position where I was paying a lot of money in taxes, I knew there had to be a better way.

I still remember where I was standing when I got the call from my CPA saying that even after making my quarterly tax payments and taking all the depreciation they could, I still needed to send in more than $370,420 to the IRS...in two days.

I began searching for ways to keep more of the money I was working so hard for. Then I read Robert Kiyosaki's little purple book *Rich Dad Poor Dad*.

After doing a lot of reading and studying, I realized I was paying far more in taxes than I needed to and I committed to making the necessary changes. CPA Tom Wheelwright from Provision taught me that if you want to change your tax, you have to change your facts.

So when I realized it was up to me and that I was in control of my outcome everything changed and I started behaving differently. Simply put, I was chased into the multi-family apartment space for tax reasons.

Investing in real estate strategically could solve my problem and provide me with not only really good monthly cash flow but also a tax shelter. Prior to this I didn't know the difference between active, portfolio, and passive income and I didn't understand how depreciation worked.

I was taught that if you make a lot of money, you have to pay a lot of tax. The truth is, you can make a lot of money while paying very little tax or no tax at all. My strategy (or really my lack thereof) had not been tax friendly. I wanted to avoid the pain of giving my hard earned money back to the government.

Fortunately, I realized that I am in control of the outcome: whether I am taxed or not. I devoted a lot of time, energy and study to figuring out how to do it and finally cracked the code.

I was consuming all of the information I could find. Quickly, I found The Real Estate Guys Radio Show podcast, downloaded every episode going back to about 2007 and listened to each one. I soaked it up like a sponge.

Robert Helms and Russell Gray "The Real Estate Guys" were incredible. I listened to their teachings for a year solid.

The Real Estate Guys had already taught me so much, but I knew they had much more to share, so I decided to attend their Investor Summit at Sea. That all-star event is where I began to learn the incredible value of getting around the right people, and where I began my career as a real estate syndicator in the multi-family space.

After buying several hundred apartment units on my own I got to the point where I needed to slow down. I was running out of my own money, but there were great apartment deals available in the market and my team was killing it. I wanted to take advantage of the opportunities.

Around that time not long after the great recession I was invited to sit on the founding board of a local startup bank, at this meeting I heard several conversations that went something like this: "I don't know if investing in a startup bank is a great idea, I may not see any kind of cash return for the first five-seven years, but it is better than putting my money in a CD."

I could not believe what I was hearing as I knew most of the guys sitting around the table. They were wealthy businessmen, most of them able to write seven-figure checks. I assumed they would all have much better investment options than a bank CD.

A few days later I had a conversation with a good friend of mine who is a local CPA. He was familiar with what I was investing in and the returns I was getting in the apartment space and he was also at those first several bank meetings. I asked him if he heard the conversation about the CD and he had.

I asked him if he thought there was a need for a syndicator to put real estate deals together for investors and give them the option to partner with me and invest for cash flow? He thought there was a serious need for that in our community, and with that I started out.

The thought of asking an investor to have me make investment decisions for them and asking them for their money to partner with me in a deal scared me to the point of sleep loss. I knew I needed to surround myself with the smartest and best people in the space.

So, back to The Real Estate Guys I went. I joined their syndication mentoring club and soaked up all the information I could. I learned a ton about what to do and, even more importantly, what not to do in my new syndication journey. You become like the five people you hang around the most, and I was around some great folks.

When I started out, like so many new syndicators, I NEEDED investors to fund my deal. I didn't have the network, the depth, the experience, or the confidence, so I really "needed" investors to fund my first deal and subconsciously acted as such.

I see this in a lot in new syndicators trying to make the deal happen. There's a lot of pressure. They don't have the leverage or the network and they need some momentum. Often, they make the mistake I did early on and focus too much on themselves instead of focusing on their prospective investor.

A great book every new syndicator should read is *The Go-Giver* by Bob Burg.

Successful syndicators break through and shine. You'll see they care about their investors. They want to make a difference, and it's not all about themselves. Always put your investors' wants, needs, and desires first because it's never, ever, ever about you...ever!

We may have multiple deals going on at the same time.... Some may have strong cash flow while others may have unique tax benefits. Still others may have low cash flow but lots of equity appreciation potential. Always learn about your investor and try to pair them up with the deal that makes sense for them and not where it makes the most sense for you.

At first, it took a conscious decision to put this lesson into action. Now it's second nature. My first syndication I was ultimately able to raise $850,000 in 45 days. Before that I had never raised a dime in my life.

People don't care what your needs are. They care about what's important to them. I quickly learned to approach things from a different perspective. Instead of desperately needing money to fund my deal I started approaching investors to present an opportunity. If a potential investor is willing, ready and able and the opportunity is good for them…now we can have a discussion and it looks like it may be a good fit.

Since 2011, we've acquired several thousand apartment units and we now have a strong portfolio of multi-family properties which provide us with lots of cash flow and tax benefits.

In 2012, a good friend and mentor of mine introduced me to a couple of guys involved in the ATM space. I started investing with them passively and it soon became one of my favorite asset classes to invest in. After being a passive investor with them for several years and getting to know them well, they approached me about joining them and becoming an active partner.

Then it became my job to go out and raise the needed funds to take down large portfolios of ATMs. In about 13 months I was able to raise more than $20 million in the ATM space. It is fast becoming one of the favorite asset classes for my investors as well.

Of course, those sales have provided financial benefits. But, it gives me the most joy when I think about each investor who I have been able to give access to really good positive cash flowing assets with really good tax benefits that they will have a great experience with and who I have given an investment opportunity outside the grips of Wall Street.

Over the last five years, my investors and I have partnered with several all-star teams. We teamed up with the developers at Mahogany Bay Village in Belize and became the largest shareholders in what is now the very first branded hotel on the island of Ambergris Caye, Belize. What started as a bare piece of land with several canals dug into it, just recently opened its doors in December 2017 as a Curio Collection by Hilton.

I used to focus on the numbers, but now it has become more about impact. How can I impact the lives of more people and how can I create a relationship that will result in a positive experience for them and their families?

When I think about the value we have created for several hundred investors, that's what gets me excited. Where once I was just a novice, now I am a mentor in my syndication mentoring group, and I love helping others be successful in this space.

The #1 thing that has been key to my success in the investment world is doing business with the right people. Most of the time when you are doing business with a great team, they will make great things happen. But you will rarely ever do a good deal with a bad team.

I like to do business with the right team over and over again because it's hard to find or build great teams who fit the bill. You don't always know if someone is going to be a great partner until you've gone through a deal or 2 with them, watched how they perform and seen who they are under stress when you run into issues.

My mentor Robert Helms says "Time will either promote you or expose you"

Over the last decade I've learned some valuable lessons and I pick my partners carefully. I don't even look at the deal first; I look at the people. The deal is only going to work as well as the people behind the deal. I don't get excited about a specific deal anymore. I get excited about the chance to do business with an all-star team.

The right people are great, competent, ethical, trustworthy, and you know they are going to do what they say they are going to do. You are setting yourself up for success by associating with the right people. When you get around great people, great things happen.

Third party endorsements from folks who I trust are huge. If someone in my network who I trust and who I think highly of will endorse a potential partner and has done a few deals with them that have worked out very well, that speaks volumes to me. When looking for a potential partner or team to invest in I look for folks who have done multiple deals with them and let them share their experiences.

So, what do you do when you don't have the right team or when you don't have the right person on the team? Cut the cord as fast as you can and get out. Most often it doesn't have to be a "burn the bridge" experience where it gets loud and ugly; it could be as simple as declining to participate in the next deal with them.

Depending on how our relationship was, I may tell them "never again." But once your partner shows their true colors and you decide it is not a good fit, just exit as quickly and gracefully as you can.

Syndication has been a very rewarding experience for me. I am doing this because we can do more as a group than I could ever achieve alone.

When we are together, we create a community. We build strong relationships. Sharing ideas and information with my community is rewarding to me. I want to get my investors on a path to success. I want to help people see things their CPA, attorney, and conventional team would not have shown them. That's how I can add a lot of value.

You can be conventional, or you can be wealthy. Pick one.

When I speak to an investor now, I am presenting an opportunity. However, I am presenting more than the opportunity for them to grow their wealth. I am offering them a chance to be a part of our club. When people work with me, they get access to more than just the deal; they also get access to my team through me. I have created a community where leveraging my network is encouraged.

My goal has been and continues to be to create an environment that is healthy for entrepreneurs and investors to get together, network, and learn together.

Every summer we host an annual BBQ in my backyard for all of our investors which I enjoy immensely. I've had people tell me they want to invest with us just so they can be invited to our annual party! It's a network of really good folks. That's what I will continue to build. Again, when you hang out with great folks, great things happen.

When you find the right people, they will lead you to other right people. When you get in the right group, in a healthy environment, with good people, good things happen. That's the power of the network. That's the power of community.

TWEETABLE
To be super successful in syndication you need to care about people. Put other's wants, needs, and desires first and you will be rewarded.

Dave Zook is a professional real estate investor and syndicator who has raised more than $70 million. He and his partners own well in excess of $150 Million dollars of real estate. He is active in the multi-family apartment space, resort property, self-storage, and ATMs and has personal holdings in multiple states and several countries. As an investment strategist, financier and author, Dave is sought after as a speaker on financial podcasts, radio shows, and live seminars.

Contact Dave and his team in Lancaster, PA for investment insights or to partner up with a winning team with a record of success. Info@TheRealAssetInvestor.com, www.TheRealAssetInvestor.com

CHAPTER 17
Freeflying
From On Top of the World to the Core of My Heart
by Sean Hutto

It was a fall day just a handful of years ago, and it was absolutely gorgeous out! The temperature was about 70 degrees, the partly cloudy skies had slowly cleared away, and I was sitting on the floor of a Twin Otter (a high-winged, twin prop turbine aircraft), one of the greatest jump ships used within the skydiving industry. It was the eighth round of an eight round skydiving competition, The National Skydiving Championships, and the medal for our division was all but locked in. It was considered "in the bag," and all we needed was an average round to earn our medal.

The plane ride was less than 20 minutes to the altitude at which we were to exit. While I usually used that time to go over the upcoming dive plan in my head, I found myself in a place of reflection, a place of profound gratitude. The last 14 years had led up to this moment. It was a culmination of 14 years of training, team building, and networking. I was so overwhelmed, feeling like I was sitting on top of the world as my dreams were becoming reality.

Imagine that you have the opportunity to learn and participate in your hobbies...your passion...your dreams...at the top levels. I was getting to learn from and play with the best in the world. It would be like a skater getting to ride the ramp with Tony Hawk himself, or a baseball player getting to practice and play with a three-time World Series Champion like Todd Stottlemyre. That is where I found myself on that day. I was discovering that there are so many levels to everything that we do. That's the type of learning that can only be discovered by hanging around with true champions who push you to stretch and grow. I had been coached by the world's best. I was so lucky! I was so grateful!

The previous year I got to be a part of the World Record Team and landed in the Guinness Book of World Records, and this year I was about to earn a medal at the Skydiving National Championships! Just picture it. You're in the magazines, you're playing with the world's best, and you are definitely living out your dreams! It was absolutely AMAZING! What happened in that moment of gratitude, in that moment of reflection, caused me to discover the one thing that changed everything.

I have had people tell me that they "heard from God." I would respectfully listen, but in the back of my mind, I would wonder, "How do you know that? Are you sure you didn't just have a little heartburn or something?" So, when I write the following, I don't take this lightly. It literally hit me like a ton of bricks. I mean, it was distinct, loud, and specific. The emotions were swirling throughout my body and my heart was pounding. I was like a junior high boy losing his girl for the first time. In fact, as I write this, I feel the tears pouring down my cheeks.... I couldn't explain it, but somehow I knew in my heart this was probably going to be one of my last skydives for a while, and a new season in life was soon to be upon me. Then, just as my emotions were going crazy, the indicator light came on telling me we would be jumping out of the plane in a short two minutes.

It was time to compose myself, wipe my cheeks dry, and get my helmet on. It was time to focus on the job at hand.

We lined up in the door and out we went.

It was a great round of skydiving. We accomplished our goal, and it felt magnificent. That night was a huge celebration. Our mentors won their division, we had our victory, and everything was right with the world.

There I was at the pinnacle of my skydiving career. I was finally getting to experience the thing I loved more than anything else in the world at a level of which I had only dreamed. And, in hindsight, maybe that was just it. It was first before everything else in my life, and I was a "taker." It was all about what I could get, what I could learn, and what I could accomplish. They say that the greatest barrier to truth is the assumption that you already have it, and a truth I was not privy to at the time was the fact that we all have a purpose, and that purpose involves what you can give back and what you can contribute to the world around you. We all play a part of a larger body and have an obligation to be the very best we can be in playing that part.

Up to this point, I had been growing as a person. I had been learning the basics of setting my mind on positive things, visualizing the right outcome, setting my goals, and learning some better habits. What I did not know is that there was a whole other level of understanding in the world of personal development. You see, I had not yet discovered that you can grow and develop on purpose, with focus. But, in order for me to get to the next level of understanding, I was going to have to lay down the one thing I loved more than anything else. I'm not saying everyone needs to stop doing what they love in order to make this discovery for themselves, but for me, what I loved was in the way of who I was meant to be (which I am only now fully understanding through hindsight).

As with many young men, there was still a lot of pride and ego at play. It's easy to mistake intelligence for wisdom, to assume that if I'm smart enough to figure out how to get through the day, surely I can get through life. But it's not about just getting through the day or getting through life, it's about contributing to life, to the lives around you, and being a part of that larger body.

I was blind to the fact that we are all changing, and by the next year I would not be who I was the year before. If I didn't pay attention, I would end up where I did not want to be, or even worse, who I did not want to be.

About 30 days after the Skydiving National Championships, I was approached by a very good friend of mine about a new endeavor in which he wanted me to play an intricate role. I had been volunteering for a local organization. It was growing pretty quickly, and needed a leader to help organize and operate a certain department. As soon as he asked, I knew this was why I experienced that distinct, loud voice during that eighth round. This would be an obligation that would take me away from the skydiving world for a while, the world I loved, but I knew that's what I was called to do.

My contribution to this organization ended up being leadership, organizational, and technical skills that I didn't even know I possessed. In fact, I probably didn't even possess them when I started out, and that is the important part of this story. It's about the growth that took place. I got to be a part of helping this organization grow from a few hundred people to many thousands of people, and it's still growing today. However, this story isn't about the organization's growth. It's about my own personal growth. It's about the discovery of change. This is my one thing that changed everything—the discovery that, if I changed, everything around me would change. I could become a greater person than I ever knew possible, discover God's purpose in my life, and give back in order to become a contributing part of the greater body of which we are all a part.

Many years have passed since I took on that endeavor. New leaders have entered the scene, and the organization continues to grow by leaps and bounds even today. I am honored to have played an intricate role as well as to have grown through the experience. Jim Rohn says, "It's not as important what you get from what you're doing as it is who you are becoming by doing it." I know that I am a better person for getting out of my own way and letting God transform my life to begin living my purpose—a purpose in helping others to discover the world of change and that if they will change, everything around them will change.

I was talking with a young lady whom I coach in a specific sales arena, and she was having a really "bad day." She had just broken up with her boyfriend, her sales were down, her clients were canceling appointments, her boss was riding her pretty hard, and life was just beating her up. I listened with an intent ear. As usual, I challenged her with some good ole Jim Rohn wisdom to not wish it were easier but to wish that she was better, and she mentioned that she was just going to, "give it all up to God." In that moment I realized one of the greatest attributes I had been practicing unintentionally. I don't have to experience "bad times" to "give it all up." I strive to be at a place of surrender at all times, and I believe this is accomplished by constant gratitude. When we walk in gratitude, we stay connected with the universe and the Creator thereof 100% of the time, all of the time. In doing so, our change is constantly directed towards our purpose, towards our destiny.

This book is about that one thing that changed everything. For me, that one thing was a moment, a moment which led to a discovery, a moment of getting out of my own way in order to discover personal development at a level that could truly help me to fulfill my purpose. I don't claim to have arrived, but the train has certainly left the station, and that is exciting!

I have grown to the point where I am now slowly getting back into the skydiving community, the community I love so much. My heart just swells as I write these words. It is amazing how much I love the people, the sport, and everything that it is. It's a family, and now I can be a "giver." I can give back to my skydiving family and the sport I love because of who I have become, and even more importantly, because of who I am becoming. There is no destination on this journey. We can never stop feeding our minds and growing. Change is ever constant; therefore, we must not get lazy in our personal development.

So, how does one discover that one thing for themselves? I believe it starts by laying it all down. Your true purpose in life is going to be a lot bigger than you and certainly a lot bigger than you are today. The only way to discover your one thing is to go on the journey of personal development. Pay attention to who you are becoming in everything that you do.

Jim Rohn said it best when he said, "The greatest gift you can give somebody is your own personal development. I used to say, "*If you will take care of me, I will take care of you.*" Now I say, "*I will take care of me for you, if you will take care of you for me.*"

I believe these are incredible words by which we all should live.

TWEETABLE
Focusing on gratitude keeps you connected to your Creator and your path of personal development directed towards your purpose

Sean Hutto has been described by peers as a "Firestarter," a person who through passion, tenacity, and leadership ignites those same qualities in others. With a background in sales and mortgage banking, he focuses on the coaching, training, and success of others. He brings this passion to all he does as a skydiver, speaker, coach, entrepreneur, lighting designer, and philosophizing student of life.

Connect at seanhutto.com or email to sean@seanhutto.com

CHAPTER 18

Submarine Commander + Robert Kiyosaki = A Formula for Prosperity

by Gary Pinkerton

In 2012 I had a two-hour conversation with Robert Kiyosaki that woke me up.

We started talking on life as a military leader, him commanding a combat helicopter crew and me a nuclear attack submarine, but turned to the failures of our school system and what makes only a few find true success. He made a comment that I had heard from him before, but at that moment, it almost knocked me down. "Everyone is a genius at something, but our school system and society only reward academic genius and push the rest into becoming obedient workers."

I had just recently left command of the USS Tucson, and I had read a life-changing book *The Creature from Jekyll Island* and spent hours with its author G. Edward Griffin earlier that day. A month before, I read Ayn Rand's Atlas Shrugged that had moved me like no book ever before, and until Robert made that comment, I hadn't known why. I was on the wrong path. I was an entrepreneur at heart who had chosen at 19 years old the safer path of getting a good education and secure job. I've always known leadership came easy to me, but I was sharing it in the wrong world. Kiyosaki's comment just then and Griffin's earlier description of a grim economic future made me realize that, like Rand's John Galt, my purpose was to help others secure their future and then perfect and share their genius, to help create a thriving America as envisioned by our founding fathers where people spend the bulk of their time on activities they're uniquely gifted to do and that they gain energy from.

I was on the right path as a child in the 1970s-80s on a small dairy farm in the Midwest. The idea of focusing on creating products and providing services for which they were uniquely gifted was practiced by everyone around me in our small agricultural town, and it inspired me. But those times were very different—high interest rates, high inflation, and a gas shortage brought scarcity and heartbreak to most people I knew, and my family was no different. We started small side businesses every time we saw a need not being filled in the community. It was invigorating and helped keep us afloat for a while. Looking back, I was clearly on the right path, but working to exhaustion with my dad every day to save the farm in that environment was not enough. I was entering high school when we lost everything. We made enough at the estate sale to pay off the loans shortly before the scheduled foreclosure, walking away penniless, but without defaulting on any promise, and that meant a lot to Dad.

Living on a remote farm, I spent almost all of my time with Dad; he was a great man, a patient mentor, and as true a friend a parent could be. I hated seeing his spirit crushed and health failing, and it gave me resolve to show him it had all been worth it; his son would be successful. Too poor for college and inspired by Dad's Army service, I got accepted to the Naval Academy. I was grossly underprepared for that first year, but with the help of some great new friends, and the vision of Dad standing next to me at graduation, I stuck with it until the instructors pulled me out of training for a call from home. Dad had been rushed to the hospital and was dead. I was crushed; my biggest goal in life and the only motivation I had for enduring Plebe year at the Academy were gone.

No one, including me, thought that I would return, but someone at the funeral commented at the right moment that Dad was watching and would still be proud. And so I pressed on.

My Navy career was personally rewarding and very successful. But I had positioned myself in the queue to be an Admiral by relentlessly chasing the wrong goal, and it almost cost me the thing I hold most dear, my family. My finish line was achieving guaranteed financial security so my family did not experience the poverty of my childhood, and I thought that could be achieved with a large net worth. I'd been exposed to Maslow's hierarchy of needs pyramid through Robert Kiyosaki's writings, but I hadn't learned what it took to meet the needs at the bottom level, avoiding poverty and having everything necessary for basic survival. I thought what it took was a big investment account. So, like many Americans playing the dog feverishly chasing its tail, I worked longer and harder, spending all of my time away from my family to cross a finish line that didn't exist: a big nest egg that would make us safe. It took me 20 years to see the truth, that a net worth of any size could be lost with a few bad decisions.

Halfway through that journey, at a crossroads of staying in a career or leaving, the answer seemed obvious to me. I should stay to get the pension and salary increases that came with promotion. When I was discussing it with my wife, she made a comment that I didn't understand for years: "Stay if you want to, but don't think you are doing this for me and the kids. We don't enjoy this life." She clearly saw I was on the wrong path, but I dismissed it as an ungrateful comment, and under the powerful fear of scarcity and loss, I stayed the course.

Another decade of this behavior had brought our relationship to the breaking point. Continuing to chase the pot of gold at the end of this rainbow meant I would be doing it alone. Reading Atlas Shrugged, time spent with Griffin, and the conversation with Robert Kiyosaki were done for survival, to hold my family together. And with Robert's comment on genius, I understood Rand's lesson taught through her character John Galt. The ability to add value to others, not large bank accounts, brought permanent safety and security, and even prosperity. People were their own greatest asset, and they achieved success and happiness by spending most of their time mastering their skills, their unique genius. Thankfully I learned that before destroying my marriage.

Finally I saw the path clearly, and I took action. I put protections in place for my family and moved our assets where they earned money for our needs so that I didn't have to, freeing up my time to discover my unique genius, plan a business, and increase my skills. As I started adding value to others, life became more and more abundant, inspiring me to work harder, master my craft, and add even more value. Most amazing was the confidence I gained. Recognizing that money came by default when I improved the lives of those around me and that my unique genius was truly valued by others, I was at peace and was extremely excited to do much more.

Today I help others get on the path my family found. I help them put in place protection and a guaranteed financial foundation as well as create passive income so they have the confidence and time to chase their dreams. Many in the middle class recognize that while they are comfortable, they are not on a path to permanent success. They cannot still be running on the W-2 treadmill at age 80. For the past 30 years, the typical advice has been to amass a huge nest egg, step off the treadmill, and carefully spend the savings. This path has been devastating for American families. Lacking the education and support from a prudent financial team, many become unable to continue working in old age and live in poverty completely beholden to social security. Most that reach their goal still live a life of scarcity in retirement because, not knowing how long the money has to last, they spend only the interest earned on their nest egg. In a zero interest rate world, that too brings a retirement of poverty. Uninspired individuals lured by the drug of comfort spend a lifetime at work, and if they can escape, find themselves in a retirement filled with constant fear they will run out of money. I help people change this story. There is a different path that leads to prosperity.

This path is not hard, it is just uncommon. Protection from financial ruin is an essential first step. It is simple to achieve, but masterfully hidden from us by Wall Street. Developing passive sources of income is the next key component. My choice has been rental real estate, but private lending, royalties from intellectual property like books and music, business cash flow as a passive investor or owner, and dividends are equally good options. The key is to have multiple streams and to focus on cash flow, not appreciation. Cash flow creates freedom to grow. Asset appreciation builds a nest egg, the old path. Gaining clarity on your unique genius as soon as possible is the third critical part. Most adults have uttered the phrase "I still don't know what I want to do when I grow up." People I knew in the military and I were saying that in our 40s. Don't wait that long; ask family and friends what you do uniquely well and what they see you doing that inspires you. Time is the only truly scarce resource; money is renewable. Buy books on the subject and hire coaches skilled at helping you discover and perfect your talents.

My purpose with this story has been to help others learn a huge lesson more quickly than I did. Every human's greatest asset is their unique genius, and sharing it with the world is the path to success and happiness. Mine is helping others put the worry over safety and security permanently behind them. Once freed from those chains, people buy back their time by creating passive income streams to meet their family's needs and to fund their pursuit of mastering and sharing their unique genius. This is the path of life, liberty, and happiness our forefathers intended, and it is not too late. To your prosperity!

TWEETABLE
Success is focusing on your greatest asset, yourself, not a W-2 or big nest egg. Share unique genius with the world for true prosperity!

Gary Pinkerton is a wealth strategist, entrepreneur, motivational speaker, and real estate investor. He uses 30 years of ethical leadership gained at the US Naval Academy and honed as a nuclear attack submarine commander to improve the lives of his clients. Through insurance-based financial products, real estate, private banking and alternative investments, he helps individuals guarantee a better future and pursue their unique genius. Learn more at garypinkerton.com or contact him directly: gary@garypinkerton.com

CHAPTER 19

How I Went From Honorary Wack Packer to Online Entrepreneur

by Lloyd Nolan

In 2010, I was finishing up my third and worst year in sales. I was driving four to five hours a day from the Bronx to Brooklyn and back home again and I was also on probation, but it certainly was not from a lack of effort. I worked hard, and at the time I thought I was working smart, but I wasn't. Looking back, I also wasn't doing anything to better myself as a salesman. Sales can have a unique way of breaking your soul when you are not doing well. I got into the position because I was a great project manager with a civil engineering background. I knew how to run a project, and I knew the product performed and believed in the product. My charming smile, blonde hair, and blue eyes may have helped me as a child model, however they weren't helping me close sales out in Brooklyn. I was getting thrown out of buildings and car dealerships left and right.

At the time I was living with my parents, barely covering my draw and partying…a lot. I had met the girl of my dreams, and looking back, I can't believe she ended up sticking with me. I had a way of not letting my friends and family know how bad my numbers were or how defeated I felt. I was in my late 20s, in cruise control in my mind and not worrying about a damn thing. All I really lived for was the weekend and where I was going to get my next kick. I was a funny bastard at the time too, thanks in part to my long commute which allowed plenty of time to listen to Howard Stern and company. I considered myself an honorary Wack Packer. I would listen to the show on the way to work, during the day in between calls, and then again on the way home when the replay came on to make sure I got everything and knew all the jokes. I knew more about Baba Booey than I knew about myself.

My brain was wired for cracking jokes, prank calls, and some interesting stories about celebrities. Now don't get me wrong, I respect Howard Stern, and still think he does one of the best interviews out there. However, this daily, consistent ritual of mine was not making me a better person, a better boyfriend, or a better son. It was not growing my sales. It was not feeding my soul.

So one day, when I was at my wit's end, Mr. Tony Robbins came on the radio during an ad and started talking to me. It was an ad I had heard a dozen times before about his new Ultimate Sales Mastery System DVD course. I was finishing up a terrible year in sales with no hope. I hated my territory, the drive, you name it. I was not in a good state. So I said to myself, "Aight, Mr. Tony "Effing" Robbins. Let's see what you got."

I called that number scrolling across the Sirius radio screen and made my first investment into my personal development. Now, I had been given books before, or I was forced to read them in high school, but I never physically took money out of my pocket to purchase a self-help or a personal development course or book of this kind prior. I was arrogant, and I thought needing help for yourself was for the weak-minded. I figured you either knew what it took to succeed, or you didn't—not the best attitude or mindset to have in life. I was a typical, young punk hanging onto whatever threads of adolescence there were still left to hold onto to. But I knew something had to be done, because I was literally at rock bottom in my young sales career. I remember the feeling I got after purchasing the DVD course. It was like a glimmer of hope had entered me, and I was looking forward to the delivery. I forget how much it cost, but it was a decent chunk of money. I was used to blowing a couple hundred bucks at the bar, so I figured it was a night out. I would just stay in one night the next week. (Do you think I actually stayed in? You're right, I didn't.) Little did I know, this purchase would alter the rest of my life.

So I got the DVDs in the mail along with a book. I went to Staples and made a copy of each page for myself, turned off Howard Stern, and popped in Tony Robbins. At the time, I had no idea what that simple purchase, and more importantly, the action of following through with the purchase and listening to the program, would do for me. Did you know that most people don't even go through the courses that they purchase? I'm sure if you are reading this, you are probably one of the few to take action and go through courses that you buy.

What I learned in that DVD course changed everything for me. It wasn't just a business breakthrough or sales. The DVD course showed me that I needed to work harder on myself than I ever did at work. That really threw me for a loop. That concept of working harder on yourself than you do at your job is a concept from the late great Jim Rohn, and he had a way of doing that to people with his simple, elegant way of expressing the English language with a twist that really made you think. Jim was a mentor to Tony and one of the main reasons Tony launched himself into becoming the machine he is today.

One of the DVDs featured Gary Vaynerchuk on stage, and he gave a presentation about turning your passion into a successful business. It wasn't so much the topic that drew me in. It was how he talked, how he acted, and what he sounded like that reminded me of myself. I couldn't believe there was this guy on stage in plain clothes cursing, being passionate, and being himself. It really resonated with me and I went all in. I took their recommendations, and I decided to model them in order to become a top salesman. I decided that in order to get out of this rut I must get resourceful. I started buying audiobooks, Success magazine, CDs, and books on sale. Dale Carnegie, Napoleon Hill, you name it, I was exploring the world of personal development every single chance I got.

Instead of listening to prank calls and whatever was going on out in Hollywood, I turned my car into "Audio University." Jim Rohn became the grandfather I never had. I listened to him endlessly. A farm boy from Idaho, as Jim liked to say, was connecting to a city boy looking to make a name for himself in the big city of dreams.

I ended up making massive changes in my life on account of immersing myself with this knowledge. I couldn't get enough of it. I was running up my credit cards because, like I said, I couldn't get enough of it. I was able to work myself out of the Brooklyn territory and into the West Side of Manhattan where I still am today because I started to get resourceful.

Now that I was able to put myself into a great territory in Manhattan, I still wanted more. I didn't want to settle for becoming the best in my company. I want to earn an additional income. Everything I had been reading at the time, every personal development teacher, when it came to money, would consistently say across the board that you need to start earning multiple incomes in order to become financially wealthy.

So, there I was again, back in my car, but this time driving to and from New Jersey to spend time with my beautiful fiancé each weekend. A particular billboard on the New Jersey Turnpike stood out to me every time. The billboard was something about not being happy with your job and making money. That caught my eye, and one day I said to myself, "Screw it. Let's do it." I called up the number and started my journey in online marketing. This was my first experience with an MLM, affiliate marketing, online business. I made a commitment to make this work. I knew I could do it. I had never really failed at anything in my life that I put my heart and mind into, but I have to admit I was in over my head.

During the time, my wife moved into my parents' house with me; we got married and conceived a honeymoon baby. I was on a roll. I took her to my first Tony event, Unleash the Power Within. Note to everyone out there: Don't drag your pregnant wife, especially if it's her first pregnancy, to a Tony Robbins UPW event and ask her to walk on fire. It may not have been the best idea, but I wanted to experience this with her. I made a commitment to hire a coach there for my business and my life. I still utilize Tony Robbins Coaching till this very day. It has helped me grow into the man I am.

I ended up not succeeding with that online company and moved to the next thing. I started up with an MLM company which aligned with my values and loved it, and then things didn't work out. I got tired of asking people to build a business by relying on their friends and family. It wasn't working for me.

When I attended Tony Robbin's Date with Destiny in December of 2016 everything changed. Again. (Are you seeing a pattern here?) I became really clear on what it was I wanted in life. Who I was pretending to be and who I wanted to be. I had a lot of internal battles going on, and I was able to get clear on who I was going to become and how I was going to do it. I was able to come to terms with the miscarriage my wife and I had suffered earlier that year. At this point in my career, I had been a perennial top 10 salesman in my company. Professionally, what I was doing was paying off, and I was thrilled with that aspect of my life, but as for my side hustle, I had nothing to show other than a blog that was mediocre at best.

That was until I came across the same fellas I worked with years ago in online marketing who were forming a new company. I decided to go all in with them. Because of my breakthroughs at Date with Destiny, I knew I wanted to start my own business and I knew these guys were the right people to learn from. Now was this a risk? Is it still a risk? Absolutely YES, but if you live your life in your parents' basement listening to Howard Stern all day isn't that a risk too?

I'm only interested in gambling on myself because I know who I am. I know my work ethic, I know what my outcomes are, I know the reasons WHY I want those outcomes, and I know the actions that I need to take. I have created a BLUEPRINT for my life.

You have to bet on yourself. You need to believe in yourself and believe that you will follow through on what it is you want in life. Living life in neutral, taking no risks can be the riskiest thing you can do.

This past year I went all in on my side hustle, this book is proof on that. I have built my own website, a blog, an ebook, and my own online product on mastering YouTube. I have my own webinar that introduces a business model I use. I had none of this last year.

You are reading this chapter right now because I met Gary Vaynerchuk at his sneaker release and got the chance to thank him for helping inspire me, to start my own journey in life, on the Tony Robbins Ultimate Sales Mastery System DVD.

That day, feeling on fire, I came home late and checked an email account I never check. I saw a subject that caught my eye. I read the email and was like, "Let's Crush This!" I responded because I was on fire. I didn't hesitate, I TOOK ACTION. I didn't care if I was going to be told NO.

That opportunity was for me to be a part of this book. And here I am, sharing my story to inspire you the same way I was inspired back when I started my personal development journey. In short, take risks and go all in on what you are great at, and don't look back. Keep putting in the work each and every day. Become more. Do more. Embrace the hustle.

TWEETABLE
Become More. Do More. Embrace the hustle.

Lloyd Nolan hit the jackpot when he married his wife and became a father. Being a father and loving husband was a lifetime goal of his. He loves working in NYC and loves his online business side hustle. Lloyd lives to connect with people. He is grateful to have the opportunity influencing others on how to take their life to the next level in all areas (physically, mentally, & monetarily). He demonstrates that through techniques and strategies concentrated in personal development and on how to build a profitable online business. If you would like to see how to take your life to the next level with Lloyd go to http://www. nextlevellifestyle.com

CHAPTER 20
A Recovered Alcoholic Carrying the Message of Hope and Happiness
by Daniella Park

I always had this vision of being a writer of action movies and landing a big role as an actress in Hollywood. As it turns out, my life turned out very differently. Now, I just want to share with you my truth: my experience, strength, and hope from a recovered addict and alcoholic. I want to share with you this very exciting journey I have been blessed with... YES, BLESSED! Learning and accepting that I am an alcoholic was the moment that changed my life forever. "Alcoholic" is a term used to describe someone who suffers from alcoholism—they have often both a physiological (physical) and psychological desire to consume alcohol beyond their capacity to control it, regardless of how it affects their life. Yes, this will get messy and very dangerous!

As a kid, I was always the kid on the block who had all the good treats and the cool parents. I can tell you, from as early as I can remember I was not such a great kid. Just very unsatisfied, discontented, and had this thing that was the "I always wanted more" syndrome. My parents were very attentive and often wondered why I was such a brat. They spoiled the daylights out of me and gave me the world, but that hole inside was never filled. When I look back now, I just cringe at some of the things I put my poor parents through. We didn't have much structure, but we had lots of money which always kept us good and busy traveling, shopping, and living the high life which fed my alcoholic "thinking" way before I ever even took a drink. Even as a child, I craved more of just about everything, so this lifestyle worked well for me.

As I got older, I wanted to finish school early and go to college. I was just sick and tired of the high school crap and was having a hard time making it to classes. I decided to take some adult classes and went to a school where I could earn credits quick and graduate with a high school diploma. My drug and alcohol addiction really took off after high school, and I was not the type of girl that could take a drink and put it down. Alcoholism is one of the leading killers of human beings in this country. I had a physical and mental allergy to alcohol. My body does not metabolize, break down, alcohol as fast as a normal drinker. This makes my body crave more, a phenomenon of craving. I lose full control of my ability to stop drinking. Yes, it's bizarre, and unless you're an alcoholic, you can't really ever understand it. If you're an alcoholic, you can diagnose yourself very easily and can try controlled drinking to see if it works for you.

After a while, I found something else more potent to numb out with... DRUGS! I say this here because my purpose in life is to spread hope and awareness that anyone anywhere can pull themselves out of the dark holes of addiction into a new world of hope and faith. We are not bad people; we are just sick people that need to get well. My addiction got so bad that it was obvious that I had a problem, and I used every day of my life for 15 years just to "feel normal." There was not a sober breath all those years. It was like I didn't know how to live, and my mental capacity left off when I started at seventeen years old. I can tell you, that's hardly living, and the things that this life brought me to in desperation just took me to my knees. I heard voices, I was paranoid, and I was living to die. But in truth, it came to be that...I had to almost die to start living again.

On September 11, 2006, everything changed. I was in the shower after a very hard night. I felt at the end of my rope with utter loneliness like never before when my body decided to fail as well. I started having horrible pains like someone was stabbing me in my stomach over and over. My hands were stuck closed, and my face was contorting. I figured this was it, I was having a stroke, and now I was going to lose the last bit of life I had: my looks. We both know looks only get you so far, but that's as far as my delusional mind could see at that moment of my life. I dialed 911 and had my mother rush to get me. We went straight to the hospital. We sat in the waiting room because there were eight other critical patients in there. I remember telling my mother as I sat white as a ghost, "I'm so sorry Mom I'm not going to make it."

My pain grew so excessive that I couldn't help but to scream. I had never felt pain like that! I went into emergency surgery. I had put a hole through my stomach lining and the bacteria was traveling through my organs, burning and making my body septic. It's a time I will not forget, thank God. I am grateful to be alive to tell my story today.

I was thrown out of the hospital and had no visitors at home except my parents. I lived this big life, hanging with movie stars, and out every night for years, and no one really truly cared about me. The life I had been living left me spiritually bankrupt.

I still wasn't mentally sober, but then something remarkable happened.

I was struck sober after a quick visit to the pharmacist to see if she had anything to alter my mind. I couldn't have caffeine, cigarettes, or pills and thought maybe she could give me some cream to make me "feel better." That gives you an idea of how an addict's mind works! Do you know what she said? "There's a 12 Step meeting next door. I suggest you go!" It finally hit me at that moment, I had a problem. I honestly didn't know…I thought I was just a bad person who was a drug addict. I never thought about getting help or that I had a disease called alcoholism!

I walked into the meeting, and an old woman in the room was crying. I ran out thinking Hell no, this is not for me. I picked up my phone and called my old drug dealer and schoolmate who I knew was sober and drove straight to meet her. She guided me my first couple days. Now I call moments like this a "God shot." Which to me is an unexplainable experience that happens beyond my power and couldn't have happened without a higher power or spiritual experience. We had been friends for over 20 years and at times we were heavily partying together, but I saw she was sober on Myspace and I still had her number.

> "…the dark past is the greatest possession you have—the key to life and happiness for others. With it you can avert death and misery for them."
> AA, 2001, p. 124

I have been sober since September 11, 2006 and work with girls of all ages to regain their lives back. Recovery is not easy, but it is worth it and being able to share my past has been my greatest asset, giving me a purpose in life. It also reminds me of what can happen if I choose to go back there. Sharing my story keeps me sober. Now that's a great deal! For fun and for free!

> "The more I shared secrets that I thought were so awful, the more people were drawn to me and I to them. I found some serenity when I got out of the driver's seat, I found God working in my life."
> – Unknown

Getting well and self-discovery has been the most exciting thing I have ever done. I had never really, honestly looked at myself. It was always everyone else's fault, and I couldn't ever admit fault for anything, ever. Getting sober, I started feeling my feelings and looking at some of my reactions to situations, past relationships, and resentments. It made me crazy to try to live with all this madness and with a stark raving, sober mind running through this over and over like a hamster racing on its wheel.

What was my solution? How would I be able to live sober with all this past wreckage still there with nothing to resolve it all? It took work, self-work.

For me, I could not do this alone. I got a sponsor/mentor to help me work through these issues and my life started to change. Becoming willing, open-minded, and honest, I was able to get through these tough issues with another alcoholic's help. I, for the first time in my life, got a higher power, who I choose to call God. This was this biggest event that ever happened to me because I learned that all my problems could be trusted in the hands of God, and that whatever happened was exactly the way it was supposed to be. That worked for me! What a total relief. It took such a heavy burden off my back, the idea that I had to manage and take on all the issues of the world. Once I understood that, we moved to work on those character defects and fears which helped build my self-esteem. We dealt with my resentments and we made amends, and I felt so free. I never even thought about alcohol or drugs! There is a solution to this problem, and you do not have to do it alone. We pass it on to keep it, join us on this road to freedom.

TWEETABLE
You don't have to cover up being an addict in recovery ever. Wear your courage proudly for what you've overcome. Clean and sober is badass!

Daniella Park is a wife, sales expert, business owner, marketer, speaker, blogger, recovery advocate, top achiever at Coast to Coast Computer Products Inc., and the creator of recovery 12 Step store and clothing brand "Doing It Sober." Growing up in Hollywood, Daniella worked as a stunt woman, stand in, producer, manager, and former Vice President of "legendary star maker" Jay Bernstein Productions. For more information or speaking inquiries: info@doingitsober.com

www.doingitsober.com
Instagram: doingitsober
Twitter: doingitsober
Facebook: facebook.com/doingitsober
Linkedin: https://www.linkedin.com/in/daniella-park-71067010/

CHAPTER 21

Finding My Mission in Remission

by Luke Moore

It was the worst moment of my life. I was 24, in college, laying in a hospital room by myself, digesting the news that I had cancer. That was a pretty rough day. I really didn't feel anything; it was an unreal moment.

My parents had not heard the news yet. They were on their way from my hometown. I will never forget their looks when they came in. They had no clue what was going on. All they knew was that I was getting a blood transfusion. Telling your mom and dad you have AML leukemia is hard. It was one of the hardest things I ever had to do, until I had to say it again two years later.

I was in and out of the hospital for over a year. It was six rounds of chemotherapy: 24 hours a day, seven days a week, six different times. I slept with chemo, showered with chemo, and took chemo everywhere I went. During the year of treatments, I had many ups and downs. It was depressing to see everyone out enjoying life while I wasn't sure about mine. It was hard to want people to visit. The last time I saw friends I was healthy, active, and had a full head of hair. It was painful, sickening, but most of all enlightening. Life is precious, and life can be taken without notice. The bad times made me really appreciate all the good times.

Growing up I worked with my grandpa a lot. I started running heavy machinery and developing land with him full time in the summers when I was 14. He is a major part of who I am today. He was one of the hardest working, most giving and honest people I have ever met. He had an old school way of telling you what he thought. He had no filter and said it like it was. He toughened me mentally and physically. I always wanted to be as great as him and treat people like he did. He passed away this year. I will never forget the values he taught me.

My grandparents, parents, and girlfriend were with me throughout everything. If it were not for my parents and girlfriend, I am not sure I would have made it mentally. They were there for me all the time and tried to keep me positive through the many dark days. They did more for me than I ever deserved, and so did a lot of others. I am very thankful for everyone who reached out and came to see me.

After six rounds of chemo, I was finally in remission. Amanda and I moved to Steamboat Springs, Colorado to fulfill a dream of living in the mountains. She completed her internship for her design degree. I snowboarded and fly-fished. After finding out we were expecting, we moved back to Iowa to begin our professional careers.

We took a weekend trip to Rochester, Minnesota for a routine checkup and camping with my grandparents. Things took a turn for the worse again.

I felt great on the way up. I felt like I was the healthiest I had been in a long time. I changed my diet and cut out junk food. I had been extremely active living in the Rocky Mountains. We were getting excited for the arrival of our baby Lily, and I was getting excited to ask Amanda to be my wife. I wasn't nervous going to that appointment like I probably should have been. I was excited to get in and out and then go revisit the areas that I once used to fish, but this time healthy and not worried about falling in the water with my Hickman line (for my IV) still imbedded my chest. Unfortunately, that wasn't God's plan for me that day.

We sat in the exam room waiting for my doctor to arrive. Amanda and I sat there talking about the trip and were excited to get out on that beautiful summer day. The doctor came in the exam room, and she was crying. I remember that moment like it was yesterday. I remember sitting there feeling bad for her that she had something that bothered her so much. Then it hit me; she was crying for me. My blood was bad again. I was in shock. We cried, and I don't remember much after that until I had to tell my parents.

Amanda was pregnant. And I was sick again. The future felt very uncertain. I made the call to my parents and gave them the news. It was worse than the first time. I remember the moment clearly. It's imprinted in my head: sitting in my truck at a stoplight crying on the phone, trying to get words out of my mouth. What was supposed to be a great camping trip with my grandparents turned into looking for housing to prepare for battle again.

It was the next day. I went to the hospital to prep for my stem cell transplant. First, they condition me with chemotherapy and full body radiation to damage and possibly destroy my bone marrow. After months on conditioning I would receive the donor bone marrow, that is if they can find a match for me. The donor marrow replaces your bone marrow in hopes of creating good blood cells again.

During all the treatments and time lying in bed, you have too much time to process. You sit with so much anxiety from the meds, and your brain races. Nothing calms it. You can't get comfortable; your legs feel like they're racing. I would get mad that this was happening to me, again. They try to calm you with medicine. The medicine works until it wears off. I had this huge weight on me that I didn't realize was there until the night my doctor came in. It was late, after normal work hours. This is either a really good thing or a really bad thing.

Turned out it was a great thing. The doctor came in and with much emotion let Amanda and me know I had two perfect matches for a stem cell transplant! It was a huge relief, the news I had been waiting for. Sometimes people don't get a perfect match at all. A match that is compatible but not perfect causes much more rejection when the transplant happens. I had two perfect matches. The second time I faced cancer still today makes me nervous to go to Rochester to get my checkup, but it was a gift. That time really made me stop and think about what is important in life.

A year after the stem cell transplant I got a job working in a production studio shooting car commercials. I just couldn't picture that was where I was going to end up. I felt like I didn't go through hell two times to do this mediocre job that wasn't fulling to me. I got the entrepreneur bite and wanted to own my own business like my grandpa and dad.

Somehow, I began apprenticing with a friend doing flooring and custom showers. When I told my doctors this, they were not happy. I had lost a lot of bone density from the radiation. I was not working with 25-year-old bones anymore and the work was demanding. I apprenticed flooring for a couple years then went out on my own. I created a good name for myself and was doing new construction houses. That led me to learning about rentals. I read and learned how to analyze a property and ended up buying my first one influenced by the flooring knowledge I had.

As I got really interested in rentals and passive income, I started reading more. I read *Rich Dad Poor Dad*. I realized I was doing many things wrong. It was at that moment I learned I could build a business that could run without me being there and do the things in life that I wanted to do.

I grew tired of flooring. I hurt. It hurt so bad to get on the floor and get back up. My knees would pop. They would ache. I needed a change. So that's what I did. I created a different business that turned over rental properties. Top to bottom, a couple guys and I did it all.

The business ran well without me. My friend and I had a crazy idea of going on a 211-mile backpacking trip throughout the Sierra mountain range. It was my first backpacking trip. We went for it and completed it in 18 days. It was unreal. Those types of moments are what I want to create with my family. After reading and learning, I found out that it is possible to make these things happen. I was starting to figure out how a business should run. It was then that the light bulb in my head went off. I wanted to create more memories like this with my family. Memories will last a lifetime.

With the jobs that I was doing, I met great people along the way and formed great relationships. These people have helped me more than I would have ever thought anyone would. We flip houses and continue to purchase rentals. It would be extremely hard to make it without the people who have trusted me along the way.

As I have continued to learn about real estate I have expanded my goals. My wife and I have teamed up to start building residential assisted living homes here in Iowa. I genuinely like to help people and provide a great product. We will be breaking ground on our first new construction residential assisted living home this spring.

Going through complete hell can teach a person a lot. All great leaders have been through dark times. I too learned how to take that and turn it into power. The feeling of the possibility that you will not be around to see your daughter grow or not get the chance to marry your girlfriend will make a person think about what is important. I remember vividly a moment when I was lying in bed. I would have given anything to be healthy. There isn't any amount of money in the world that will fix you when you're down and out. You must have control over your health and take care of your body. Without health, there is nothing.

There were parts of treatment which were so terrible I would rather have done anything else. Chemo injected into my spinal column was my least favorite. It was not only unpleasant during, but additionally, each one came with a migraine that lasted a week. It was moments like those that today make me better at facing tough situations: situations where you would rather be anywhere else. You cannot do anything but take them straight on. They will pass. It will get better. I always keep that in my head. No matter how bad it is, it will pass if you take it on. It may be a workout that you're about to do or a big mistake that "was caused" at work. I take it straight on and get through it.

All the trials I have been through make me move faster to get to my goals quicker and to keep making new goals after I accomplish the first ones. Time waits for no one. Don't wait to start your dream. No one knows how long their clock will tick. Don't wait for the perfect time. That time is now. I have a fire lit within me that can't be put out. I have a sense of urgency to keep moving. If you keep waiting to start what you really want to be doing in life, you could be too late. There are many things in life worse than failing at trying to accomplish your dreams.

I live the lessons I have learned today. I have formed great relationships without which I wouldn't be able to do any of the work I am doing today. It was ingrained in me to be an honest, hardworking, courageous person. I owe that to my dad and grandpa.

1. I have learned to celebrate in the good times and learn in the bad times. I have had a lot of victories and defeats. The problem exists, and so does the solution.

2. I have learned that I owe everything to my family and friends. During my entire life I have had help from so many people building real relationships has been so powerful. People I have met, worked out with, and shared a beer with have helped me get to the path I am on today. I would never be where I am or be going where I am headed if it were not for great relationships and my family.

3. I have learned how important the bond between my spouse and me is. I firmly believe we all need help every step of the way. I needed the assurance from my wife that this is what I should be doing now. The strong connection and faith in me allows me to go after my goals and dreams.

TWEETABLE

All great leaders have been beaten down and broken. Rather than blaming, learn to leverage the dark times into power.

Luke Moore has been investing in real estate since 2011. Practiced in buying rental property, flipping homes, and new construction, Luke's wife Amanda and he are now building the first of many residential assisted living homes. With two young children, they are focused on building residential assisted living business in and around Cedar Falls, Iowa for the foreseeable future. To connect and share ideas with this couple, email Luke@blueinkproperties.com.

CHAPTER 22

A Near Family Tragedy Helped Me Change How I See Investing

by Tyler Gunter

They said, "Here's your son, Dad" and suddenly, just as quickly as they said that, he was passed through a little window into the NICU. And his younger sister followed just moments later. I just stood there, helpless, not knowing what to do or how to help. I was staring at my wife laying there on the operating table, our twins were now in the hands of strangers, and I had the sudden realization that nothing was in my control.

My wife and I were elated and somewhat terrified when we found out that our family was growing by not just one, but two new babies. All of our plans were out the window. She wouldn't be going back to work as we had planned, but would now be staying home to care for our babies. Then to add fuel to the fire, Tamra was put on extreme bed rest at 10 weeks. That made me the sole provider for the family, and things were going to have to change drastically. How was I supposed to provide for all four of us? She wasn't able to work anymore at all. I thought I had nine months to figure this out!

I had always wanted to be a real estate investor. It was now or never. Tamra and I took five thousand dollars that we couldn't spare on new credit cards to hire a coach. I was still working and Tamra was on bedrest, so she would do the "homework" as I called it. We had weekly meetings with our coach and he was holding us accountable to not only our realities but also our future dreams. We went through the six-month process, digging deep into how we spent our time, where our earned income was being allocated, and how to narrow down and find the right real estate deal. We learned so much in those six months, but in the end, I still didn't have an answer to how I was going to provide for my new family. How would we maintain our current standard of living?

As the months continued to tick by, we got serious about finding our first deal. In a somewhat sarcastic moment one night, I asked Tamra if she would start making some phone calls on local property listings. She told me that she would like to watch me make a call first as she wasn't sure exactly what to say. (She knew. She just didn't have the confidence in herself yet.) So I took the listings and made a call to the first property I saw. A friendly voice answered on the other end, and within a matter of minutes, I had learned what expenses I could expect and a general idea of what to expect in rent and general care. Tamra had just been released from bed rest, and we were both eager to get out of the house, so we agreed to take the 20-minute drive out to look at the property and meet the sellers that night.

As we rolled up to the property, we were excited and a little nervous. After all, this was our first real attempt at being real estate investors. We toured the home, a 3 bedroom 2 bath unit on a rented lot. The current owners had been planning to retire in this home and had done a lot of improvements. Tamra and I left feeling great about the opportunity and came up with a game plan on the drive home. We called the owners right when we got home and made the deal. I laughed out loud in somewhat of a smug tone saying, "See honey, that's how it is done from start to finish." Our first property was under contract. We were doing it. However, it was becoming painfully clear that this one property cash flowing $185 a month was not going to solve our financial problem.

We were two weeks away from closing on our first rental home when Tamra started talking about pains she was having in her stomach. We were more than two months away from our due date; this had to be Braxton Hicks contractions. We figured it would pass. After about an hour of trying to relax, playing Cashflow to distract ourselves, they were becoming more regular and increasingly painful. We kept telling ourselves this couldn't possibly be her body preparing to deliver the twins. We tried several home remedies to relax her body and calm the contractions. However, when I was able to start telling her when a contraction was going to start, we knew it was time to go to the hospital. When we were checked in, Tamra was in full blown labor at only 31 weeks. She was given all sorts of drugs to try and stop the labor and speed up the development of key organs for the twins little bodies, but coming from a small rural community, there was only so much our local hospital staff could do. A Life Flight helicopter was called in from the University of Utah Hospital with two highly trained NICU nurses and incubators on board just in case of an in air delivery. I don't think it had hit me yet how serious the situation was, even as I helped the medical staff load my wife onto the helicopter and raced home to grab what I needed to make the three and a half hour trip through the night to get to the hospital she had been flown to.

The team at the University of Utah Hospital were able to hold off the birth of our twins for five days. Tamra, unfortunately, remained in labor for that entire time with constant contractions. I was traveling back and forth from work while Tamra was in the hospital. She was calling regularly with updates, and I was traveling up to see her as best I could every couple of days. One day as we were joking about the adventure we had been on to this point, Tamra had a major contraction, the largest one she had experienced since they calmed them five days prior. The nurses had monitors connected all over her body measuring contraction strength as well as the twins' heart rates. When the doctor came in to check and see what was going on, his facial expression said it all. There was no more waiting; our babies were coming today. Our son was in position, but our daughter was breach and given her tiny frame (only 3 lbs at time of birth) they were concerned about a natural delivery and the risk of injuring her or Tamra trying to turn her. So an emergency C-Section was scheduled within 20 minutes. The problem was that Tamra had been on blood thinners to protect her from clotting as she has a rare blood disorder. She couldn't go into surgery within 12 hours of taking her medicine, and it had been given to her only a few hours prior. The decision was made that the surgery had to happen to save Mom and the babies, and they would have to deal with the hemorrhaging if it became an issue.

Because I was traveling back and forth for work prior to the birth of our babies, Tamra had handled all of the legal documents, including the forms explaining everything that could go wrong, on her own. Having never gone through a major hospital procedure or the birth of a child yet, I was blissfully ignorant. Looking back, I am still astounded at just how incredibly strong and brave Tamra was in that moment. She knew her risks, what having the twins so early could mean, and what battles lay ahead. Me? I took for granted that everything was going to be fine and we would all be together shortly in the birthing room, cuddling and sending selfies with all the details of our babies' births to all of our friends and family back home. Little did I know, I had a tremendous amount of growing coming my way in just a few short minutes.

Tamra had already been moved out of the room so that she could be prepared for surgery. One of the nurses dropped off some scrubs for me to change into and told me to bring a camera if I wanted to document any of the process. I can still remember standing in front of the mirror, staring back at myself all in blue with a hair net and booties over my shoes in pure elation thinking that I was about to be a daddy. Then, one of the nurses came back in and asked me to follow her into the operating room, as they were about to start. When I entered the room, I wasn't prepared for what I saw. While Tamra had spent the better part of the last week being plugged into machines, this was different. I was watching each of her breaths on a monitor along with her heart beats and blood pressure. I can still hear the sounds of the alarms and the frantic voice of the student esthetician as he called for assistance every time her heart rate dropped or she would shallow her breathing. This was the moment in time that I look back on and gather strength from. Having seen what she is capable of and knowing that she is on my side through everything, I know that together we can accomplish anything.

As I was finally grasping the gravity of what was happening and the risks that my new family was in, I heard the doctor say to me, "Here's your son, Dad." Then he was gone to the NICU, then my daughter. My wife was hanging on, but I was no surgeon. Nothing was in my control. I was scared! More scared than I had ever been in my entire life. More scared than the first time I told my wife I loved her, or that moment I took a knee in the cold snow to ask her to spend the rest of her life with me. More scared than the moment we bought our first home together, or switched jobs. More scared than I could ever imagine.

These are the moments I grew. Suddenly life wasn't scary. Entering the entrepreneur world didn't seem as crazy. It didn't matter about our financials or lack thereof. Everything that had been keeping me up at night over the past seven months seemed so distant. The only thing that mattered in these crazy minutes (and the following two months of intensive care for our kids) was my new family. I was going to be there for them no matter what. I wasn't going to miss out on anything.

I stayed with Tamra as they continued to make sure all was right with her and sew her back up. We were transferred to a recovery room where we sat for what seemed like an eternity. I still hadn't been allowed to see the babies. Tamra had been struggling to maintain her breathing after the surgery, and I didn't want to leave her side. My emotions were all over the place. I didn't know where I was needed most when finally Tamra turned to me and told me to go be with the babies, that she would be fine.

As I walked into the NICU for the first time I was guided to the level one section. This was for the highest risk babies. Nothing really prepares you to walk into a section of a hospital specifically designed to house a large number of tiny babies all hooked up to oxygen with IV's everywhere and alarms going off. Nothing prepares you for that moment when things go wrong for the family sitting right next to you. As I was enjoying my first contact with my son, the man next to me was saying goodbye to his. In that moment I realized that I had been taking life for granted. I was just along for the ride. I was just a passenger, going where life took me. I just assumed this whole time that all would be well because it always had been. Tamra would deliver happy, healthy babies, and we would go home and ride the ride. This realization changed everything including the course we would eventually take.

My babies had ventilators on, IVs taped to their heads, wires plugged in all over their bodies, and the tiniest diapers you could ever imagine that they were swimming in. I reached into each incubator, and each of them immediately grasped my finger. In that moment I knew we were going to be okay.

We still had an uphill battle, and my babies had to fight hard to survive those first two months. I was a commissioned salesperson, so if I wasn't working, I wasn't providing for my family. Thankfully I had an amazing boss that knew, as I had recently discovered, the importance of family, and I was able to squeeze a week's worth of work into Monday through Wednesday and spend the rest of the time back at the hospital with my family. Those two months taught me about our ability to let go of things that are out of our control and to trust in the universe to handle them while I focused on what was really important. I learned that NOTHING could stop us when we knew what we wanted and where we were going. Once I finally knew my true WHY, I knew what I was capable of and that I could overcome any obstacle calmly as long as my WHY was in focus.

My feet were in the fire, I had been tested beyond any other trial, and we had come out okay. It was with this confidence and with knowing that no trial in life will ever compare that I was able to adjust our focus from single-family housing to purchasing our next rental property: a mobile home community with 33 spaces and over 24 homes. We still didn't have any money at the time, and we were barely making it paycheck to paycheck. I had to go out and ask for every bit of the purchase price (a little north of a million dollars.) The banks weren't interested in financing mobile homes, so it had to be private money. I wasn't afraid of hearing the words NO anymore. When I was met with a no, I just moved onto the next opportunity and made the deal happen. With one transaction, a whole lot of faith, and the understanding that we could make it work no matter what, we had now not only replaced Tamra's income that we had lost during the pregnancy but also mine. I wasn't yet 30, and I was looking at our financials and realizing that I could retire if I wanted to. If I hadn't had my feet to the fire with my wife and kids in the hospital like that, I never would have had the drive or the faith to go out and make this deal happen. No trial seems insurmountable anymore.

Our twins are now six years old, and one year ago we added one more beautiful daughter to the mix. They are all healthy and amazing. We have since built and sold a ground-up facility maintenance company and acquired an insurance office utilizing this same concept. The insurance office was a newly discovered passion of mine sprung from the birth of the twins. With over $600,000 in medical bills from their birth along with the costs of traveling back and forth and keeping Tamra a place in Utah for the two months, I got to see the ugly but also the good of insurance. My passion became sharing the amazing benefits and the unknown secrets of making insurance work for you. We are now expanding our offices and our online services nationwide with the same vigor and courage we set out with in our other ventures.

The day I almost lost my new family I learned to have faith, to let go of what I can't control, to trust that the universe will handle what I can't, and to focus only on what is important in that moment and time. Don't fear change, for a change in the plan can take you places you never thought possible.

TWEETABLE
I had been tested beyond any other trial and survived. With this confidence and knowing that no trial in life will ever compare, I moved.

Tyler is first a loving husband and father and then an award-winning financial advisor, Insurance specialist, real estate investor, and serial entrepreneur. Tyler focuses on helping others live a full life by focusing on financial planning and insurance strategies for the now, the future, and their legacy. Tyler encourages investing to better your life now as well as into retirement and offers unique strategies to help anyone.

Tyler@priorityplusinsurance.com
775-738-7131
Facebook: trgunter

CHAPTER 23

Facing the Moment Changes Everything
by Greg Zlevor

It took three minutes for it to happen. I was standing in a room facing 30 people who did not want me there. They worked for a large automotive company that was spinning out one of their divisions. For this group of employees, nothing was certain except this: there would be layoffs. People were anxious and upset. Morale and productivity had stagnated. So the company hired me to run a series of workshops to help them deal with the shift.

"Let's start with introductions," I said in that first workshop. The participants were seated in a horseshoe formation, and I stood at the center of the open end. All eyes bored into me. "Please introduce yourselves and tell me a bit about what you do at the company."

One by one, they did. Everything was going smoothly until—

"This is total bullshit," said the guy in the middle. Sitting there in his jeans, flannel shirt, and hat, he stared me down angrily. "I shouldn't be in here with you fancy consultants, with all the effing money you're charging us. I should be back in the shop proving my value and doing my job, and I think you've got no effing idea what we're going through."

The room fell silent. Everyone was looking around as if to say, "Holy cow, we're three minutes into this and already there's a confrontation!"

I paused for a long time. Thirty sets of eyes watched, waiting to see what would happen next.

The way I saw it, I had two choices. I could challenge him right back. Or I could embrace the moment, no matter how uncomfortable it was.

"You know, thank you," I finally said. "Thank you for being honest. Because if we can't be honest, we can't get anything done here."

There was another long pause, and then I took a breath and said, "Next."

You could have heard a pin drop.

That was the moment that changed everything—not just for me, but for the outcome of that workshop. It spurred people to deal with the real issues they needed to face. And it ultimately made our time together a success.

But it wasn't a once-in-a-lifetime moment. As we go through life, each of us encounters moments like these over and over again, whenever we are challenged, shamed, or confronted by a strong personality as I was.

And when that moment arrives (as it always does), here's what most people do: they run from it. They try to ignore it, explain it away, or throw the blame back at someone else.

But real power lies in saying yes to that moment. Not as an agreement. Not as a concession. But as an acknowledgment. As I discovered, if we rise to the challenge and embrace rather than fear those difficult moments, true change begins to happen.

What does that look like? Simply put, accepting the moment means saying, "Yes, I will stay open to what is being said, even if I don't agree with it." It means saying, "This happened. I didn't want it, I may not like it, but I'm not going to run from it."

These moments may seem insignificant, but they define us as people. They define our teams and our organizations. And based on how we respond, these moments have the power to cut through chaos and conflict and spark real community.

In my work, I always come back to this concept of community. It is at the heart of everything I do as a leadership consultant. And I was lucky to discover what true community really looked like very early on in my life.

I will always remember the one time that my dad looked at me with an expression of mild surprise and even disdain. My brother was getting married, and there seemed to be absolutely no limit on the guest list. In my mind, it was spiraling out of control.

I confronted my dad. "Are you going to set a limit? You have to think about the venue, the meals to order, the plans you'll need to make. Where do you draw the line with all this?"

I came at him with all the logistics and none of the heart. I was thinking about plans. But he was thinking about people.

"Greg," he said, giving me that look I'll never forget, "there are no lines."

"Everyone who wants to come to the wedding will come," he said in a whisper of exasperation. "I'll work out the details. There are no lines."

And this is how my parents lived their lives, with this simple and generous philosophy: there are no lines. Everyone is welcome, and we're going to make it work. When I was growing up, our house was the center point between the high school and the grade school. Between four boys, someone was always coming over to stay with us, and my parents welcomed them all with open arms.

My dad fondly recalls Saturday and Sunday mornings counting heads to see how many eggs to scramble and pancakes to cook. Over thirty different people lived with our family at one point or another, including a Catholic priest who had little money, my seventh-grade basketball coach who had lost his job, a brother's friend who was experiencing difficulties at home, a horn-playing summer exchange student from Germany, and so on.

Our home wasn't very big, but the welcome people received always was. (In fact, we had one tiny bathroom. It was so small that you could turn on the sink faucet and bathtub while sitting on the toilet!)

My parents embodied the true spirit of community. As I grew, went to college, and started my career, I was fortunate to encounter more examples of what true community looks like. I found it during my summers in a Christian community in Canada and in the years spent running community-building workshops under the wise guidance of Dr. M. Scott Peck whose books, The Road Less Travelled and The Different Drum, inspired me to walk down this path.

Through it all, I have come to understand that humans have a real hunger for community; we are drawn to it, we yearn for it, and we feel the loss of something undefinable when it is missing. True community is the place where we can thrive, but also where we must be challenged. It is extremely valuable, not only to individuals but also to organizations. Because when you strip an organization down to its essentials, you are left with a group of people in search of community.

The companies I work with never say it that way, and they may not even see it that way, but that is what it is. Companies are looking for community. They will say they want their people to work together, to communicate better, to create team synergy, and to lead in ways that matter. They will call it stakeholder engagement or getting buy-in.

All those things are worth cultivating. But without real community—the glue that holds everything together—none of them have true staying power. They fall away as soon as a leadership initiative or consulting engagement is over.

When you create real community, everything changes and almost anything becomes possible: people look out for each other, they support each other, they're engaged, and they do incredible work together. If your company is also a strong community, you are unstoppable.

Recently, a client did an analysis of an eight-year leadership program we run for them (a Fortune 50 company). Of the leadership program participants, 84% still work for the organization. The norm is 65%. This represents over $25 million in savings. Community is valuable. People stay with and for each other.

But creating community isn't easy. In fact, it's one of the hardest things you could set out to do. It requires those hard confrontations and disagreements. It requires authentic, open communication—even when it's painful or difficult. And most of all, it requires saying "yes" to the moment.

It always comes back to the same moment.

Leaders who respond to these moments wisely are rewarded with engagement versus mere compliance, or worse, chaos. And they can make wiser decisions because they know how to be in the moment without being threatened by the moment.

How do I stay connected with people and possibilities in the moment when I am getting exactly what I do not want?

What happens when leaders can't handle the unwanted moments?

I was once invited to work with a company that had just hired a new CEO. They called him "three-wall" because as soon as he arrived, he built walls between himself and everyone else. The old CEO had worked in a large room with about 100 other people, and anyone could walk up to his desk to talk.

But the first thing the new CEO did was build walls: one for his area, one for his secretary, and one for himself. And the walls he erected weren't just physical. In a company where the exchange of ideas and feedback had once been fluid, things began to stagnate. People lost their voices—and the company, in turn, lost valuable insights. Most crucially, they lost their sense of community.

So they brought me in to see why productivity had fallen off a cliff. I interviewed all thirteen members of the executive team as well as 30-40

140

other employees. Almost every single one of them said, "I don't have a voice. I don't have access. My opinion doesn't matter anymore."

Everything they told me pointed right back to the new CEO.

I took all their comments, prepared the report, and gave the CEO a heads up: "Hey, I'm going to share this with the executive team, but I think that you and I should walk through it first."

"No, no, no," he replied. "Just bring it to the meeting. I don't need a briefing, and it's OK if we all see it together."

I slept on it for a night or two, but in the end, I thought that he really needed to see it.

So I called him up again.

"Look, we already had this conversation," he said, getting annoyed, "just bring it to the meeting."

So I printed up the 40-page report and passed it out to everyone at the meeting. Right there, in the first couple of pages, it said, "People here don't have a voice." And I stated the reasons why.

"What!" said the CEO. "People don't have a voice?"

He turned to the first person to his right. "Bob, this report says you have no voice. Do you feel like you don't have a voice?"

And Bob said, "No, no, I have a voice."

"Kathy, do you have a voice?"

"Yes, yes, I have a voice," Kathy said.

The CEO went around the whole room, and every single person said, "Oh, yes, I have a voice, I have a voice, I have a voice."

Then he turned to me.

"How can you write a report like this when everyone here says they have a voice? This is horseshit!"

And he threw the report down and stormed out of the room.

Instead of embracing the moment before him, he literally ran from it. If he had just been able to say "Yes, I hear you, and I am here for this," everything could have been different.

I was never able to help that team or that CEO or that company. The CEO did not want what he needed. The Executive team was not courageous enough to speak up and break the "walls."

Today, I teach leaders to face difficult moments with wisdom and to ask, "What is the message here? What do I need to be hearing?" I run several leadership programs for major global brands, and during those programs participants work on real world, high-stakes projects. To succeed, they need to transform from a loose-knit group of participants to a close-knit community.

But along the way, of course, they experience conflict. They get frustrated, they get angry, they get into it with each other. And that's ok, because it's a natural part of what it takes to build a true community—a community where the conversation is real and the connections are real as well.

I coach them through this process and I show them how to wisely face their "moment that changes everything." I tell them, "Don't run. Don't hide. Don't fight. Never turn away, because the moment you do, you lose. You lose out on your future, your possibility."

I am proud of the work I do with these leaders and of the results they get for their companies. But the thing I'm always most proud of is how, after a project is complete, they look around and discover that they have built a true community.

It's an incredible thing to witness, and it all starts with practicing the attitude of saying "yes" to the moment—especially the difficult and challenging ones.

Practice. Say yes. Never turn away. In this angst lies all your possibility.

"Is it not incredible, that in the acorn something has hidden an entire tree?"
– Mary Oliver

TWEETABLE
Creating community requires open communication—even when it's painful or difficult. Most of all, it requires saying "yes" to the moment.

Greg Zlevor is the President of Westwood International, a consulting collaborative that's reimagining what it means to lead wisely in a global age. Westwood's signature, global-scale action learning programs and leadership initiatives have energized global brands like Johnson & Johnson, Kimberly-Clark, Volvo, and General Electric. How can we help your team lead wisely? Send a note to Greg at gzlevor@westwoodintl.com or call 802.253.1933.

CHAPTER 24

Three Words That Don't Define Me

by Tina Radick

My secret of 24 years that I'm about to share with you, I kept secret until now was due to many factors, as you will learn as my story unfolds.

It was 24 years ago when something I thought was a curse turned out to be a blessing in disguise. It was 1994, and I was married five years to my high school sweetheart with a beautiful two-year-old baby boy named Bryce. I was working at my dream job at the time, Clinique cosmetic counter. One day I was applying makeup on a nice lady when, all of a sudden, my vision went blurry in both eyes. I thought, *Oh I just have a piece of makeup in my eyes or something.* So I completed the makeover, and it was luckily time to go home.

My vision was not any better that evening, so I made an eye doctor appointment the next morning. He dilated and looked into my eyes with his scope. Then, within seconds, literally, he said these exact words, "YOU HAVE MS and you need to schedule an appointment with your primary doctor immediately."

My husband at the time and I were in complete shock. I vividly remember us going to my parents' house right after the appointment. They both said, "There's no way you have MS. How can he know that by just looking into your eyes?" The looks on their faces were of utter shock because I know in the back of their minds they didn't want to believe it was true nor did I. They knew I was very upset by what I had just heard, so they didn't want to upset me more. They said, "Oh honey it will be okay. We don't believe that doctor. He does not know what he is talking about."

From that day forward I never told anyone but my then husband and later my current husband. My parent's reaction was a major factor in my decision to keep things a secret. I did not want my family and friends to be concerned about me. I never was the type of person that liked to be pitied for anything. And I never wanted to be looked at differently in my personal or professional life. I have heard others on many occasions say, "Oh, he or she has *that.*" and every time they had a look of pity on their face. This is what I did not want. They did not know what they did not know.

I made an appointment with a doctor who set up an MRI of my brain and neck. When the results came back, I was praying that it was not MS. But, the original eye doctor with a horrible bedside manner was, in fact, correct. MRI scan confirmed I did have multiple sclerosis. Although only a couple lesions detected on the MRI, it was official. I had multiple sclerosis at age 24. I had multiple sclerosis at age 24 with a two-year-old child who from day one I said I would always be there to love, teach, and protect. "How was I going to be able to do that now?" I thought to myself. That went through my mind over and over. I thought that I was officially going to die young or be in a wheelchair for the rest of my life and not be able to take care of my precious little boy.

To say I was terrified would be an understatement. I was scared to death of what I did not know. I went home and cried, feeling pity for myself and thinking of the worst possible scenarios. The only person I ever knew that had this was a father of a co-worker I worked with at Clinique. He had the most severe form of MS, and every time I had seen him, he was always in a wheelchair looking frail. Without the knowledge at the time, I thought that was going to be my future. What would I do? I had a two year old that needed his mom that in the beginning kept playing like a horrible dream in my head.

It scared the living hell out of me, until one day, after wallowing in my own pity, I decided to gain the knowledge I needed whether that was going to be good or bad. I researched everything I could on what this diagnosis consisted of from A-Z. And I searched for what could be done to stop this chronic diagnosis from further progressing. I found that taking action to gain knowledge set my mind at ease. What I learned was it was not a death sentence. Fortunately, I and others can go on living a normal, productive life.

I remembered that I first had signs of MS at 19 years old. I had numbness in my hands and feet and went to many doctors. They told me nothing was wrong with me, that I was too young and that I was being paranoid.

I can remember when Montel Williams the talk show host announced he had MS for the last twenty plus years and looked healthy. No one would have ever guessed he had MS. I am sure he had some of the same feelings I did about how others would react from their lack of knowledge.

Fast forward from the first medicine that came out in 1996 to today, there are so many new medicines that are extremely effective in stopping the progression of MS. I am truly blessed and thank God every day that I am one who has had very minimal incidents or side effects. Knock on wood is what I always say. This has taught me to be grateful for what God has given me, even with having multiple sclerosis. I know that might sound strange to some, but no matter what your circumstance it truly is your attitude and how you choose to react. We all have one life. No matter what side of the tracks we are from, we are thrown curveballs at some point in our lives. Obviously, some curveballs have more spin than others. My belief is that I could have kept wallowing in my own pity of "why me" or I could have done what I chose to do: live the best in life I possibly can without worrying about what I cannot control. I choose to focus on staying healthy, positive, and working hard to be a better version of me. Not only for myself but most of all my two loving sons, beautiful step-daughter and supportive husband. I will never stop trying to make an impact and a positive difference for my family and others. To me, there is no better feeling, and I am most satisfied when I can help or guide someone in a positive way.

For the last fifteen years I have owned a successful real estate appraisal company, and for the past four years, my passion has been being an entrepreneur with many new irons in the fire. One incredible opportunity came to me through a global e-commerce company where I have the ability to do business in 25 countries. The opportunities are endless—I have been able to meet and take pictures with President Donald Trump (like him or not, he's still the president). Also have been very fortunate to lock arms with two former MLB pitchers, one three-time world champion Todd Stottlemyer and TJ Mathews who is also a champion in his own right. As Jim Rohn's quote says, "You become the average of the five people you spend the most time with."

What I learned from these champions that are now great friends is, the sky's the limit. The only ceiling all of us have is the ones we put on ourselves. We all have one life. Make it your best life. I try to make an impact on someone every day, even if its a smile or hello. Those do not cost a dime and are simple things that could make someone's day. Never let the opinions of others affect you. They are theirs to keep and not yours to worry about. Don't ever wait. The time is now to take action on whatever it is you dream of or desire because tomorrow is not promised for anyone.

I have MS, and that does not define me. Having MS has actually been a blessing to me. I look to each day as an opportunity to live life to the fullest, push past my fears to keep pushing myself to create more so I can help others who are less fortunate.

TWEETABLE
24 year secret: it's time to share so others in similar circumstances may too see their blessing in disguise.

A 15-year real estate expert, Tina Radick has a real passion for being an entrepreneur. Through ACN, a global e-commerce company with a 25 year track record. Tina has found abundant satisfaction and enjoys leading others to create their desires. She has proudly met President Donald J Trump through this company and has the pleasure to work with, not one but two, former MLB champion pitchers Todd Stottlemyer and TJ Mathews. She has a very strong belief in staying humble and kind. She has great pleasure in lifting others and finding gratitude when it seems impossible. Email tina@key2residual.com

CHAPTER 25

Going from Victim to Thriver
Removing the Shackles of a Victim Mentality
by Daniel Schaffer

The chase was on! I scrambled down the stairs into the basement two at a time, sprinted through the family room, into the hall. I could hear him right behind. I didn't dare to look, that would only slow me down. I was almost there, at the end of the short hall I turned right, I could see the bathroom now, the safest room in the house, if I could just make it there, I would be safe. I bolted in, flung the door shut behind me and grabbed the doorknob with both hands. The door didn't have a lock, but as long as I kept that handle from turning he couldn't get in, and my mom would save me.

This time was different, I could feel him struggling against the handle, and suddenly there was a CRACK! He kicked in the door. I was going to die.... He grabbed me and pushed me up against the wall just as my mom made it into hallway screaming to leave me alone or she would leave him. He cocked back his fist, hesitated a moment, then punched a hole in the wall right next to my head.

We can't control what others do to us. There are many things that happen in life that are unfair. While some of these things may appear as simple speed bumps, others can leave ugly scars on our souls that we will live with every day of our lives. It is our response to these things that truly defines who we are as individuals and what we can accomplish when we stop existing as victims, soar past living as a survivor, and begin to truly live as a thriver.

I am a Master Mentalist. I perform for corporations and colleges across North America. I am married to my beautiful wife, Cassie. Life is wonderful, business is booming, but just a matter of years ago, this was not the case. I am an adult survivor of child abuse, an addict in recovery, and for most of my life I simply existed with no upward mobility. I was living with open, festering wounds on my soul, doing very little to improve my circumstances, living off of government aid, and absolutely miserable until the one thing that changed everything happened in my life.

To understand where I am now, I need to tell you about where I have been. My wounds began around age seven. I had a neighbor who lived across the street. He was a couple years older than me, and looking back, he had obviously been abused by someone else. He had a game he would play with me called torture, the details of which I will not go into here. This was my first experience with sexual abuse. This abuse wreaked havoc on my childhood. I was too ashamed to tell anyone what had happened, although after a couple months my mother suspected something and forbid me from going back over there. Unfortunately, the damage was already done.

It was shortly after this that things on the home front began to deteriorate as well. My father always had a short temper and was very prone to emotional and physical abuse. As I began to act out, this abuse escalated. This created the perfect trifecta of trauma: sexual, physical, and emotional.

It was at this time that I discovered the art of magic. I learned that I could influence the world around me, create illusion, and even manipulate circumstances. This became one of my escapes. At the age of 10, I felt life was so terrible that I attempted to take my own life, something I didn't tell anyone about for years.

By the time I was in high school, the doctors were sure they had it figured out. I had bipolar disorder. They put me on heavy medication and told me that this was as good as it would get. It wasn't until 10 years of changing medications and dealing with horrendous side effects later that I would learn I had been misdiagnosed.

After graduating high school, I went straight into college because that is what I believed I was supposed to do. I took a break to go on a two-year religious mission but was sent home six months early after I had a PTSD episode that left me vulnerable and open to a sexual assault by a trusted friend. Not long after being sent home I sank into a deep depression and developed a severe behavioral addiction to cope with my situation.

The combination of mental illness and addiction froze my life. The best way to describe it was that it felt like the world continued moving around me and I was just stuck in the same place. I attempted to continue my education and failed spectacularly, racking up massive student loan debt only to medically withdraw from half of those classes after falling behind with cycling depression and hypomanic episodes. I wasn't satisfied with my life but had no idea how to even begin to make a change. At this point in my life I was living as a victim. This lasted for a few years during which I changed my major four times. The thing about living as a victim is that nothing ever changes. The world continues to move around you, but you remain stuck.

In June 2014, I lost my minimum wage summer job. I was taking summer classes, and they wouldn't work with my schedule. This was the first step

150

in reclaiming my life. It was the final bump before I hit bottom. I didn't know how I was going to be able to pay rent, or buy food. I went to the soup kitchen for about a week, and each day I looked around me and saw the direction that my life was going. I knew one thing for certain, that is not where I wanted to be.

Magic had saved me in my childhood, and it was about to save me once again as an adult. I went out onto the streets of Salt Lake City that Saturday with a deck of cards, a rope, scissors, a handkerchief, one fifty cent piece, a Tupperware container, and a piece of cardboard that said College Fund.

I spent the day out on that corner doing magic for those who walked by as my Tupperware filled up again and again. At the end of the day I counted my tips. $170! I was rich! Well, not rich, but I certainly wouldn't end up on the streets. I kept half for rent, and with the other half I purchased a business license, a second-hand blazer, and a top hat to replace the Tupperware. I repeated this every weekend for the rest of the summer, each time reinvesting half of what I made to get better gear, better outfits, and to put together a show that I could sell. Three months later I had booked my first children's show. I knew this is what I wanted to do with my life. Now that I knew it was possible, I set my sights to become a full-time professional corporate magician.

From that moment on I put everything into my business. Every semester I took classes that would benefit me such as video production, acting, broadcast journalism, psychology, business, and more. I noticed I had an aptitude for Mentalism, so I began to pursue it vigorously. Things were finally going well, or so I thought.

As my business grew, I came up with plans to increase marketing, reach businesses, and grow into the corporate market. What I found was that, even though I had started a business, and it was growing, I was still living with a victim mindset. Any time something happened, I took it personally and turned to my addictions and unhealthy coping strategies. It was like climbing up a steep hill and every time I slipped I let myself slide backwards several feet. Things quickly began to fall apart. With everything from my past still unresolved I had gaping psychological wounds that caused fluctuations between hypomania and depression; on top of that my addiction began to run rampant to the point that something finally had to give.

I dropped out of school and worked a second job, spending every spare second of the day either working on mentalism or engaging in my addiction. It became a vicious battle to see which one would win. I was determined in my business, but my victim mindset and mental illnesses kept me a slave to my addiction. Deep inside, I truly hated myself. I didn't know who I was, not really, and I was afraid to see who that person was. Because of this, I wore my on-stage persona as a mask in my everyday life. I was determined that nobody would ever see Daniel Schaffer. When they met me they would see the magician, the mentalist.

Because addiction is a progressive illness, with the unresolved trauma, it eventually won the battle. I would stay up until four or five in the morning and sleep until five at night unless I was working or performing. Once this happened, the work stopped coming. At this moment I realized that I was so unhealthy and so addicted that the only thing I really cared about in life, my business, was in jeopardy. I finally admitted that I needed help. Once that happened I decided to check into rehab.

The lessons I learned in rehab changed my life. It was there that I learned the one thing that changed everything. I did not have to be a victim. I could learn to be a survivor.

I was in rehab for about two and a half months. During that time I learned several important things. I learned that I had post-traumatic stress disorder and borderline personality disorder from my past abuse. I began to love me for who I was and not what my skills were. I began to see who I was underneath all my masks. I learned how to forgive myself, and most importantly, I learned that I did not have to live life the way I was living it. I was living as a victim. The world was acting upon me. The way I was living, I simply existed in that world, living day by day with no hope for the future. I learned that with hard work, I could reclaim my life and begin to truly live once again.

The facility I went to banned me from doing any magic while I was in treatment. This forced me to be myself and to see everything that made me who I was: the good, the bad, and the ugly. I began a therapy called eye movement desensitization and reprocessing to treat the PTSD, and I began mindfulness and dialectical behavioral therapy to treat the BPD. While I was in therapy, I was able to come off all my meds. After two and a half months I was cleared to reenter society. It was time to apply what I had learned to real life.

Reentering society from a rehabilitation clinic is a very interesting experience. I had a new perspective on life, I was clean and sober, and I was starting to love myself. I was receiving proper treatment for my mental illness, but having only been gone for two and a half months, my entire unhealthy lifestyle was right there waiting for me with open arms. This was the ultimate test.

After leaving rehab I took inventory on my life and business. Previously I had felt victimized by the world, and every action I took was defensive.

When something unfortunate happened I would get angry, and instead of working through it, I let it stew inside of me. I had started my business as a reluctant entrepreneur; I started my business out of survival and continued it because it had become my identity. Upon taking inventory I was able to learn the deeper reasons for my business. I loved helping other people. As an entertainer I could help others by giving them an hour they can forget about the world and feel wonder.

My new outlook had immediate impacts in my entire world. Three months later I met my beautiful wife. Within six months I had tripled my business, quit working on the side, and began to work my business full-time. Our main goal was no longer just to survive. Now, our goal is to sincerely help others, and in the process to thrive. This has opened new connections, philanthropic opportunities, and even paved the way to write this book. Being able to overcome that victim mentality and truly begin to live as a survivor changed everything. When you refuse to be a victim, your life will change just as it did for me.

There are many ways that we can be victims in life. Some of you reading this may have suffered grave injustices or abuse, others may feel victim to a demanding boss, social injustice, politics, body image, or little things like getting a bad grade in school, getting cut off during your morning commute, missing a promotion, losing a sale, or a myriad of other reasons. All of these things can hold you back in life when you let them turn you into a victim. When I was a victim I felt like the universe owed me. I felt like one day everything would change as the great cosmic scales finally tipped to my favor. Because of this I didn't put in as much work as I could have. I didn't make an effort to change my life. If you find yourself in a similar situation, it is time to get a new mindset.

Forging a new mindset doesn't happen overnight. For me, it took a long time to finally learn that lesson, and once I did, it took a lot of energy to apply it to my life. I found that when I let other things in life dictate my actions and emotions, I made myself a victim. A survivor can brave an experience objectively while remaining in control of emotions. This allows them to remain clear and focused.

For those of you who have experienced trauma, being a survivor rather than a victim may require asking for help. There are those out there that are trained to help you reclaim your life. There is no shame in asking for help because once you get it you can begin to control your destiny. Severe trauma can cause changes in the brain; these are actual changes that can require advanced help and therapy to be able to undo.

Becoming a survivor is the first step in rejecting a victim mentality, however, I am not content to simply be a survivor. I refuse to spend the rest of my life simply surviving, my goal is to not be a survivor, but to become a thriver. Here is what I am doing now.

Change the Things You Can and Let Everything Else Fall Into Place
Realize that there are things in life that you can change, and there are things that you cannot. There is great wisdom in the AA serenity prayer that says "God, grant me the serenity to accept the things I cannot change, the courage to change the things I can, and the wisdom to know the difference." When you recognize what you have power over in your own life, and stop worrying about the things you don't, life becomes much simpler. As you change the things you have power over, everything else begins to fall into place.

Look for the Good in Life and Others
What you focus on in life you will attract more of. If you focus on negativity, you will reap negativity. Likewise, if you spend time each day looking for good in others and the world around you, your mindset will begin to change. Focus on positivity, and you will find more positive influences come into your life. As you surround yourself with these positive influences, you will notice yourself taking on positive qualities in your own life.

Get to Know Yourself
Find out who you truly are, not who you are when you are at work or with friends, but who you are when you are alone with your thoughts. Activities like journaling and meditation can help you find who you are and help you unravel complex emotions related to events that make you feel like a victim. As you better understand yourself, you will be able to regulate your emotions allowing you to weather any situation.

Learn to Be Lucky
Luck can best be defined as the moment when preparation meets opportunity. Plan for the future, set goals, invest in your life, and constantly be looking for ways to improve yourself. As you do this, opportunities will inevitably come your way. When they do, you will be prepared to seize them.

Never Give Up
Change is hard. If you find yourself slipping into old habits, just pick yourself back up and keep moving forward. Setting short and long-term goals and evaluating your progress will help you keep on track as you create change in your life.

Changing your mindset is a difficult task but is worth the effort. When you allow yourself to be a victim you will experience little growth or upward mobility. As you seek to adopt this mindset in your life and business, you will remove the shackles that hold you back and will open the way for massive personal and professional growth. Learning to live as a survivor changed everything for me, but I'm not content to stay a survivor, I am determined to become a thriver and finally live life to the fullest as my true authentic self, experiencing life and helping others in ways I would have never even dreamed to be possible.

TWEETABLE
Stop living as a victim and begin to live as a thriver.

For more information about Daniel Schaffer visit www. TotalMentalism.com

Daniel is a Master Mentalist with over 20 years experience. He uses his skills and personal touch to masterfully entertain and motivate while helping businesses connect and engage with their employees and customers in meaningful ways. His goal in writing this is to offer hope and to help others who have been through similar circumstances. No matter where you may be in life, you can always improve. For keynotes, consulting, booking inquiries, more information, and video of performance, visit www.TotalMentalism.com

CHAPTER 26

The Engineer Who Escaped the Rat Race and Achieved Escape Velocity

by Lane Kawaoka

I walked the linear path for much of my life. Raised as part of the disappearing "middle-class" programmed me to study hard in school, checking the boxes on extracurricular activities, cramming for the SATs, and getting a high GPA to get into college, all to live a "practical" life. Growing up, we were told to "waste nothing" and turn off the lights every time you leave a room. I still feel guilty to order a soft drink at a restaurant as opposed to tap water.

In college, while other cohorts were playing Frisbee in the quad, I was stuck in the basement of the industrial engineering lab. Why was I not playing the sun? Because Google told me what the highest paid undergraduate professions were. Driving on autopilot for much of my early twenties, I went for a higher-level master's degree and tested to become professionally licensed as an engineer for the job security.

Upon entering corporate America, I spent my first five years of my career working for a for-profit, private company as a construction supervisor managing a bunch of entitled journeymen who were older than my parents. Facing the rigors of junior level employment, I played my role as the young guy, traveling 100% of the time for my company, sacrificing quality of life, as I navigated the operational clusters, toxic management, and other backstabbing pawns in the company.

I have a lot of scar tissue from that decade of working for the man not to mention building someone else's dream. You tell me how engaged you would be if meeting protocol was to sit next to your superior and not speak unless directly instructed to or if you were asked to address a director two levels up by mister or misses!

One day an internal company email went out notifying of a friend/ex-direct report had died in a work accident. My boss was uncompassionate about the situation, looking out for the big bad machine first (mostly his annual bonus and agenda). This really put things into perspective for me.

As a corporate road warrior, it was novel being on company expenses all the time and maxing out on airline and hotel points, but you can only have steak and lobster so many times.... The only people who cared about my platinum status were the other suckers in first class who were working for the paycheck or an acceptable quarterly review. Although I am grateful that I had a well-paying job post-2008 recession, I traded the most important resource, time, for money.

The linear path instilled delayed gratification, living below my means, and an overall scarcity mentality of saving money instead of earning more, being more. I was entranced by the pervasive Wall Street marketing to blindly put money into a company sponsored 401K plan only to "hope and pray" that compound interest would carry me to a secure retirement.

Let's not even talk about the student loans I had....

I knew where this path was going...I mean I did the math and it told me so. This is my story of how I freed myself financially, how I took ownership of my life's direction, and the series of events that allowed me to find my calling.

Seeing the (Economic) Matrix

A steady diet of ramen noodles and a free birthday latte per year made it possible in 2009 to purchase my own home to live in. Being a bachelor who was only home on the weekends, I realized that having this large home was a waste of money. I made a decision to rent it out and became a real real estate investor. You might be thinking that this was the big change, but at the time it was simply a lot of beer money after collecting the rents and paying the mortgage.

I don't know if it was the beer or being love drunk with cash flow, but I opted out of the linear path in my early twenties.

From that point on I devoured podcasts, books, and online forums on every keyword iteration of passive real estate investing. At a few hundred dollars of passive cash flow per home, the process was simple, buy a rental property where the income exceeded the expenses and mortgage, then rinse, wash, and repeat. Like a space shuttle that accelerates through gravity and escapes the atmosphere into zero-G, this was my way to financial freedom. Up to that point, the biggest breakthrough in my life was discovering the .MP3 format that compressed and played music digitally in my teens. Using this intellectual technology, I progressed intentionally to eleven rentals in 2016.

At that time, a few of my friends wondered why my ramen noodle diet was being replaced by Starbucks coffee and yummy double bacon and egg breakfast sandwiches. They wanted a piece of the action too. Duh, it was about time seven years later, said the little red hen who did all the work by herself.... As much as I liked helping people, I got tired of answering the same questions. So what does any other late Gen-X/Millennial do but start a blog? Unfortunately, the words I write, even if spelled correctly do not usually make proper statements in English, so I uploaded my *Simple Passive Cashflow* podcast to iTunes where I could ramble and honestly talk about what I was going through as an investor.

I began living more consciously, opting into more meaningful engagements with people and projects, and searching for meaning and purpose. I was beginning to ask myself, "after sitting on a beach with my unlimited supply of piña coladas and time...then what!?" Needless to say, my motivation for working in the hostile work environment that I once tolerated dwindled, so I switched to work in the non-profit public sector. I started to see the economic "matrix" where people essentially trade time for money and the rich let others build their dreams.

Being an introvert, it was paradoxically energizing to see my audience grow as I began in-person meetings and online groups I sponsored. I provided hundreds of free coaching sessions to guide newbie investors. With my engineering background and a little "bro-science," I saw patterns arise in the stories from well-paid professionals who were led into an unfulfilling lifestyle unaligned with their passions. Abolitionist Henry David Thoreau said, "The mass of men lead lives of quiet desperation and go to the grave with the song still in them." People do not have any time to look inwards and are constantly living with anxiety and self-doubts because they are working like machines in order to meet their basic needs without the freedom to find their true passion.

Why did so much hard-work lead to financial scarcity and lack of fulfillment?

This self-selecting group of hard-working professionals searching for more all had a common thread. A moment that pushed them over the edge and made them realize that the path they were on was unacceptable.

These are some of those tipping points:

- Seeing younger, less experienced workers being "red-circled" as future management and advanced through the company "fasttrack"
- Being fired to cover up shortcomings in a budget
- Internal theft by upper management

THE ONE THING THAT CHANGED EVERYTHING

- An affair by a superior lead to bankruptcy of a startup company affecting many innocent employees

- Chronic drain of working with deadbeats

- Getting lost in the office politics of getting your objectives completed when they do not align with your boss' objectives

- A retirement party for a coworker is catered with crappy Chinese noodles due to the cost control

- When you don't get the job because you do not have enough grey hair

- Because you have too much grey hair

- Being criticized for not being business savvy from those who live paycheck to paycheck (when you have a personal portfolio of a few hundred rental units)

- Sitting through endless meetings that should have been sufficed with an email

- Circle jerk meetings where the boss' dumb ideas are exalted by their minions

- When your boss with no technical experience misuses terms like artificial intelligence, big data, machine learning, and deep learning

- Being enslaved with the "golden handcuffs"

- Seeing an ambulance come to the office routinely during layoff season

- Being around the negative W2 worker speak and adopting the prevailing victim mentality

- The road warrior gets an early quit on Friday only to see the spouse at home with the pool boy

- Watching your friends receive the Seiko stainless-steel watch retirement gift

If you have found a calling in something you are good at and truly love doing it...clap, clap, good for you. Keep doing what you are doing and consider yourself lucky. If you relate to any of the moments above, read on.

The One Idea

My online journal resulted in many emails of gratitude and acknowledgment because I was empowering people with the "how to" and inspiring them to take a leap of faith to change their financial life forever. I suspect the most effective part of my message was showing people that if little, awkward engineer me could do it, how bad could it be?

I started up-leveling my peer group, and through osmosis, this brought me to a Tony Robbins event where I literally walked on burning coals! There were a multitude of top-down and bottom-up techniques Tony Robbins spoke about during the intensive four-day event. One of those lessons was "things happen for a reason," and boy, was I glad I did not leave to use the restroom when he outlined the six human needs:

1) Growth

2) Contribution

3) Significance

4) Uncertainty

5) Certainty

6) Love and Connection

Here was the game-changing moment.... Tony Robbins said, "The most important thing is contribution because the secret to living is giving. If you catch onto that, you start realizing that there's nothing you can get that comes close to what you can give. Life is calling all of us to be more than just about ourselves and that is when we get that spiritual hit."

Apparently, Mr. Robbins did not endorse the mission of sitting on a beach with an unlimited supply of piña coladas and taking food porn pictures while gallivanting the world as a tourist. Nor did he support playing it safe with a bunch of passive investments.

Later that Easter, I was baptized, and the message there too was "go forth" and help others.

Then another of my mentors, real estate legend Robert Helms, said, "When you are successful you have an obligation to send the elevator back down." I made it to my penthouse and now I and this elevator are heading back down to get folks!

We all have a finite time on Earth and an empty canvas to create a legacy. This was my one shot! Opting out of the linear path was not about getting financially free and sailing off into the sunset, but it was about standing up for change and creating the greatest impact!

The fan mail all followed a common thread of pain. Many hard-working professionals who are busting their butt on the linear path are being misled down a comfortable life of un-fulfillment. Many of them were enslaved by the "golden handcuffs," running in the hamster wheel of the day job working for someone else. Some, like doctors, lawyers, dentists, accountants, and engineers make more money to get the big house and nice car, but in the end, they are just a bigger hamster. The dogma of the Wall Street "buy and pray" method is a cover up to insidiously steal investment returns from the people who are doing all the work.

Life is a three-phase screw job:

Phase 1: You enter the workforce with the worst jobs with the lowest pay. Time is abundant.

Phase 2: When marriage and kids enter the picture (and ailing grandparents) this is the time when one should be excelling at their time-consuming career. Money is abundant.

Phase 3: Your teenage kids hate your guts and your health starts to fail. Time is abundant.

The Next Chapter

My mission is to teach and empower good people to realize the powerful wealth-building effects of real estate so they can spend their time on more important ventures and passions instead of working long hours and worrying about their financial troubles.

In real estate we use leverage, and by teaching others, I am leveraging other people to achieve their financial goals in hopes that they too will send the elevator back down for the next person.

SimplePassiveCashflow.com seeks to educate those looking for diversification and better returns outside of traditional investments such as mutual funds and stocks. This is part of a large effort to redirect billions of dollars going to the corrupt Wall Street roller coaster and help the shrinking middle-class find safer and more profitable investments in projects that benefit Main Street such as affordable workforce housing rather than luxury housing for the rich.

The true meaning of wealth is having the freedom to do what you want, when you want, and with whom you want. Building cash flow via real estate is the simple part. The difficult part occurs after you are free financially to find your calling and fulfillment. But that's a great problem to have ;)

TWEETABLE
Professionals busting their butts on the linear path are misled to a life of unfulfillment, entrapped by golden handcuffs in the rat race.

Lane Kawaoka owns over 1,000 rental units. He lives in Hawaii and works as a professional engineer with an MS in civil engineering.

Lane partners with real estate investors by curating opportunities in the "Hui Deal Pipeline Club" where his investors know that Lane has skin in the game.

By reverse engineering wealth building strategies the rich use in the SimplePassiveCashflow.com podcast, Lane helps thousands get out of the rat race, one free strategy call at a time. Email Lane@SimplePassiveCashflow.com!

CHAPTER 27

The Truth That Lies Behind My Eyes

by Denise Marie Rose

After having written this, I am feeling so inspired that all I want to do is dance and run naked through a field of wildflowers. I have so much energy racing through my veins. I feel alive. I want to be unstoppable and never look back. My journey is my passion. My children are my magic. I want to lead by example to show them that any and all dreams are possible! I dream to feel love and feel alive. I vow to treat others the way I want to be treated. If it is meant to be, it is up to me.

Now, I choose to take responsibility and I choose to feel free. Every direction I look there is another opportunity in front of me. Most all opportunities have a price tag on them, and with each one, I am faced with another decision: Do I dare to jump all in or go back behind closed eyes and tell myself freedom is not possible? My mind and self-talk have been the most negative villains in this lifetime. The conflict between love and my self-worth is my worst enemy.

The moment that changed everything is happening again right now! When I committed to this opportunity to bare my vulnerabilities; I had no idea how my life was going to be impacted, how this process would open my eyes. Over the past weeks I have reflected over the course of my life, and one layer at a time I have processed deeper and deeper.

On the surface, the events of my life are unremarkable. I have spent my lifetime sugar coating and hiding behind my smile, all while my tragedies have left me feeling suppressed like a caged bird.

In my mind I journey back to 2010 when I lost my home, when I lost my husband, and when my four children and I were homeless. For a brief moment, I see how in the blink of an eye everything changed. In 2010 I learned my own strength and grew immensely. I began to stop feeling sorry for myself and embraced my adversity. With the grace of the Church, who offered a hand up and housed me and my children, I set out to become a nurse and earned my associate degree in applied science.

But there is more to process. I still feel a void, knowing I must go deeper. Through all of the difficult, self-destructing years leading up to that; I then think that I must write about my abusive marriage of ten years. As I peel back that layer, I feel the pain and total disgust. No one deserves to experience the horror of verbal and physical abuse the way I did.

Yet another layer needs to be filtered. My mind journeys backwards as I rewind time. So many pivotal moments, bearing children, dropping out of high school, and looking for love in all the wrong places, flash back in my memories. All I am wanting to remember are the positive times, and yet so much pain and heartache take over. I stumble back to a time when I was a five-year-old little girl. In this moment all of my senses are in overwhelm.

The layers I have been peeling back are of a rotten onion! Senses in full flight and my body paralyzed, I falter. The odor smells of death. My eyes become floodgates. My tummy cringes as I regurgitate in my mouth. I am cold and begin to quiver. The pain is unstoppable because my heart is abandoning my body. As I feel my heart tear and rip from my chest then go adrift, a placated numbing comes over my soul. I remember the silence that came over me as my innocence grew dark.

Two neighborhood boys that my family trusted to walk me to and from school took advantage of that trust and allowed their curiosity and desires to overtake my body.

That night I laid restless and so very frightened. I could hear my parents off in the distance and dishes clanking. I remember the stern voice of my father telling me I better go to sleep. Shame and guilt took over every ounce of blood in my body and I began to cry. I was frightened to tell. I was young and I knew what took place was wrong. I felt so alone. I felt so dirty. I remember laying there and fighting back tears just so I could close my eyelids. Anxiety taking over I could not lay still. I knew I had to tell. Conjuring up courage, I got out of the bed. I crept into the kitchen and felt the cold flooring on the bottom of my feet. Anticipating a scolding from my father, with my tears rolling down my face, my quivering voice began to tell my parents what had happened. I remember my mother saying that she was not mad at me and that I need not worry. I remember her walking me back to bed and telling me that she loved me.

From that moment on, not another word was ever spoken of what had happened, not by me nor my parents. Life still went on and I still walked to school with those boys. Life seemed exactly the same. The only thing that had changed was me! I was not the same happy little soul. I stopped playing with others. I kept to myself and my imagination. I felt humiliated and I thought that my parents' silence was a display of their disappointment in me. The boys still full of life, were out playing in the neighborhood. I watched from the window. I began to get angry as I thought I was the only bad one. I was too scared to go outside, and they were free. I felt imprisoned and had no one to talk to other than myself. My mind took over and the confusion and self-lies began.

The message I learned repeatedly growing up was, "Treat others the way you want to be treated." My young mind tangled this idea with my feelings and misconstrued the true meaning. I spent most of my life until recently repeating this phrase in my head like a broken record. I was suppressing my hate and rage, trying to please others. I never wanted anyone to feel the way I had. I became extremely codependent. I was going to be somebody and save the world of heartache and pain. I tried to have a great attitude, and I went out of my way to give to others; even when it left me empty and broke. Round and round and round, my life consisted of just me, myself, and I behind my closed eyes. I just had to escape my mental anguish! I was done with my own self-loathing and putting everyone first, before truly taking care of myself. I learned that it's okay to get lost, it's just not okay to stay lost. Hope is home. Faith is freedom.

I relate to a lot of pain in this world, but I use my optimism to move on to the next day. I used to be burdened by self-talk that I am less important and that there are far worse adversities and tragedies in this world. I have tried to keep my composure. I have tried to be nice and giving. I have tried so hard to treat others the way that I want to be treated. I want to be loved. I want to feel safe in my own skin. I want peace and joy for myself and others. I want freedom. I want for my own children to feel protected and loved.

Becoming a nurse has granted me such confidence and has strengthened my endurance. I am learning to truly be in service to others, and I have a greater appreciation. I am a proud mother leading by example and I still choose to make a huge difference on this Earth. I start with myself, then in my own home, and then embarking on this world one life at a time.

Recently I have become an entrepreneur. I own my own global business with the largest direct sellers in telecom, energy, and other essential services. I am in love with what I do and am excited about the endless possibilities of all that it has to offer! I am embracing this opportunity and using it as a guide for opening my eyes and opening doors to make differences in others' lives. I am passionate about redirecting abundance in cash flow towards many other dreams and desires. Closest to my heart is a non for profit in remembrance of my little brother Billy. Angels of Hope and Action has a mission to serve and unite others that struggle with pain and addiction in support of transformation and rehabilitation back into life without faltering to addiction.

My quality of life has come full circle, and I have a love and understanding for mankind like no other. I am patient, I am kind, I am a Woman who stands on her own. My conviction of love, honesty, and integrity is a constant reminder to me that I am never alone.

All of these years of suppressing these emotions and telling myself that no one loves me and that I am not important has resulted in an ugly manifestation in my choices of relationships. I truly desire to connect with others and to have friends. I am shy, and learning to reconnect with myself. I must be gentle with myself if I choose to allow others to come in. I am brave, and I do choose to jump all in. My conflict has been thinking I am so different than anyone else. My heart has always known that my sins have been forgiven. I must embrace everything in my past and forgive myself. By hearing the truth one may feel a little pain, but by being honest one has everything to gain.

I am blessed and thankful through all of my confusion to have found myself once again. I no longer have to keep quiet about where I have been in fear of who I may hurt. This was a prison of my own creation. I have opened my eyes and set myself free.

Hello you beautiful world!

TWEETABLE:
By hearing the truth one may feel a little pain; but by being honest one has everything to gain.

Denise Marie Rose is an entrepreneur, mother of six children, nurse, and founder of a non for profit: Angels of Hope & Action serving and uniting others struggling with pain and addiction. As an international business owner she brokers telecom, energy, and other essential services supporting Project Feeding Kids, which feeds hungry children every time a new customer is acquired and pays a bill. She shows families another way to save money and create financial freedom.

Angelsofhopeandaction@gmail.com
Webstore: wearetheroses.acndirect.com
Wearetheroses123@gmail.com
Or Text SERVICE to 314-249-3311

CHAPTER 28

Perseverance
The Last Frontier
by Jason McWhorter

I had great role models for parents. They taught me the meaning of hard work, they taught me right from wrong, and they kept me on a path towards success. Don't get me wrong, I wasn't the perfect child that followed their advice all the time. I tried their patience and made choices that weren't always aligned with their views.

Even so, I graduated high school and shortly after decided to join the Navy with my best friend, Mark. Mark and I were best friends since grade school, and at the age of 18 we were ready for adventure and to see the world. Making this decision, I felt like I was finally in control of my future and that anything was possible.

Reality quickly set in though. My best friend had just been sent off to boot camp, and I was to follow when I got the unexpected news that the Navy could not accept me. I was denied due to the metal plates in my arm that repaired a broken bone years earlier. For the first time in my life, I was told I couldn't do something I wanted to. I was devastated.

For the next few years, I followed a path that had no real direction. I got a job in the construction field. My boss, Barry, taught me that with hard work and dedication you can accomplish anything. It was a life lesson that I needed to be reminded of. I worked that job, some days sunrise to sunset and learned a lot. Still, I had that desire to see the world. I decided to move to California. Life in California was good, but once again I found myself working in construction and just not really finding passion or focus.

Then, at the age of 20, with my entire life ahead of me, I received a phone call that changed my world. My girlfriend called to tell me she was pregnant. I was going to be a dad.

From the moment my son was born, my top priority became a long-term vision to make sure that this child would have the best life possible, and that I would be the father that his son could be proud of. This was the day I learned the meaning of perseverance. I made the decision to do something and keep doing it till the end, even if it was hard.

My girlfriend and I had some irreconcilable differences, and so we parted ways. Adjusting to life as a single dad was challenging. No longer did I have just myself to think about. Every decision I made now affected someone else. I made sure that I kept the promise to always be there. I had a visitation schedule for when I could spend time with my son, and although it was never enough time, I always made the best of it.

I began dating a single mom. We had the same values, work ethic, and most importantly, the desire to be there for our children no matter what. We married a few years later and bought our first home. I started my own construction business. Life was good. It was at this point my persistence would be tested again.

My son's mother called. This time she told me that she was moving to Alaska. Her husband was in the Air Force and was being transferred. They were leaving in six weeks, and of course, she was taking my son with her. To my disbelief, I had no legal recourse to stop her from doing this. So I was faced with a life-defining moment. Do I see my son a few weeks each summer? The answer was NO! I would not let him think that one of his parents only saw him when it was convenient.

Our only choice was to sell everything we owned and move to Alaska. Making this decision was not easy, but it was the only one that allowed me to keep my promise to my family that I would always be there for them no matter what. So we embarked on a journey that moved us 4500 miles from home. We settled into our life in The Last Frontier, and for the next three years, life again was good.

But as everyone knows, in life we are always faced with trials and tribulations. Some are small, and others test our faith in the greatest of ways. Once again, I got a phone call. This time they were being transferred to an Air Force base in Louisiana but on a temporary order that would be less than a year. So I faced the daunting task of once again making a long distance move. Could my family make another move?

Fortunately, my employer valued my hard work and dedication to the company over the past three years, and I was given a transfer to a job in my hometown. It was on faith alone that we made the move. My home was now a 10 hour drive from my son, but holding true to my promise to never leave him, we made the trip as often as possible. I knew spending that time with my son, wife, and daughter was the most important thing I could do. The following year my son moved back to the town I was living in. I thought I had won the race. After four years of sacrifice and perseverance, our family was back together and living a normal life. But my race was not over yet.

Reflecting on the adversities I had faced, I believed I was capable of being someone greater who had more to contribute. I began looking at starting my own business again. I had a great corporate job, but I just wasn't satisfied with the corporate mentality, the income limitations, and a schedule that someone else set for me.

I set out on the road to business ownership. This road would continue to teach me the meaning of perseverance. Along with my great success also came great obstacles and disappointments. This is to be expected when you own a company. I had to stay true to my belief that to win the battle you can never give up. I knew that I was only limited by my own beliefs. During the 2008 financial crisis, my business was greatly impacted. I made tough choices on the direction of our company, but I always made those decisions with the determination that quitting was not an option. I made it through that tough time, and in the end, my company was thriving. I was committed to success.

As my children continued to grow up, I realized I was becoming complacent as a parent and as a husband. Sure, I was at home at night and went to their sporting events, but I wasn't what I had envisioned I would be. I thought back to what I promised myself I would be. The commitment I had made to my business was costing me my family. It was a cost that I wasn't willing to pay. I began praying for a change and looking for a better way. Once again, I was going be taught the lesson of perseverance, only this time, by someone I had never met.

I was introduced to Todd Stottlemyre through my good friend TJ Mathews. Todd was a three-time World Series champion, and since my favorite sport is baseball, I jumped at the chance to sit down and talk to him. Within a few minutes, I knew he was someone I could learn a great deal from, not just in life but in business as well. Todd was as successful in the business world as he was on the baseball field. He was a true champion in all aspects.

From Todd, I learned the most valuable lesson in my business life, the concept of residual income. It was the first time someone had taught me that I could work once and be paid over and over. All my life I was trading time for money and then more time for more money. His lesson on residual income forever changed the way I work and do business. It was the answer I was looking for, the solution to getting back time with my family.

My road to success was once again a bumpy road, presenting many challenges, obstacles, and disappointments along the way. But I was more determined than ever that this was the path I was going to take. Todd was instrumental in guiding me down the path, mentoring and advising me, always by my side.

The change in my thinking has allowed me to pursue other business opportunities that continue to add to my financial success. Only this time my success doesn't come at the expense of my family. After all, wasn't that the promise I made so many years ago? To be there for them no matter what. The lesson of residual income has now allowed me to pursue my dream to see the world on a larger scale, and this time I'm not going alone, I get to take my family with me.

Perseverance, for many, is lost to the idea that quitting is easier. I am blessed to have learned differently. Perseverance allowed me to find success when others said it wasn't possible. It has given me the gift of time with my family and allowed me to be able to give that same gift to others. As I reflect back on my life now, I know that everything happened for a reason. Every lesson and hardship taught me to persevere. I have been able to achieve even more than I thought was possible. I now have the ability to be the best version of myself. And for that, I am forever grateful.

"...let us run with perseverance the race that is set before us."
– Hebrews 12:1

TWEETABLE

Perseverance, for many, is lost to the idea that quitting is easier. I am blessed to have learned differently.

Jason is the Founder and CEO of NextCard Pro. At a young age he developed the skills necessary to become a successful entrepreneur. With over 25 years experience in both corporate management and business ownership experience, Jason's purpose and passion now lies in helping others develop the mindset and skills necessary to become successful entrepreneurs themselves.

Contact him at jason@nextcardpro.com.

CHAPTER 29

Giving Thanks to All Our Amazing Angels

by Brad Roberts, MA

Asking the question "what's the ONE thing that changed everything?" invites us to begin searching back through our lives. As I began to search for my "one thing," my mind started reeling, images flashed in a rapid-fire sequence, thoughts passed in and out of my consciousness almost too quickly to grab hold of long enough to ponder before they were replaced with the next thought, and the next, and the next. This kaleidoscope of images and one-liner aphorisms competed with each other, appearing and talking over each other all at once.

So I dug deeper, to remembering conversations I'd been privileged to be involved in. I felt I was getting slightly closer. Soon that morphed into searching for the meaning behind those interactions, and then to searching for the feelings that those interactions evoked. I wanted my answer to the question of this book to be truly authentic to my own life, but I also wanted it to serve others and help them.

Then, one evening sitting in silence in front of our Christmas tree, my journal and pen in hand, the colored mini-lights providing the only light in the room, I just let the thoughts come...and I found my answer.

In short, the one thing that has made all the difference in my life is that I've been blessed to have some incredible people intersect my path at just the right time. A minute earlier and their impact wouldn't have been welcomed by me because I wasn't ready. A few seconds later, and well, it might have been too late.

Yet, it's much more than that. The one thing that made all the difference was that I was open to the moment, to the message, to the coaching, to the feedback, to the gentle nudge back on course offered by someone who cared. I was open to the interaction that somehow (re)directed me away from troubled waters and onto something new and exciting and scary and rewarding all at the same time. I call these individuals angels.

Let me share some examples from my life in hopes that you can relate, and find some angels in your own life.

My first angel was my grandmother—my mother's mother. I called her Nana, although she was practically my mother because she raised my younger sister and I. Nana lived with us, and it was Nana who was there to drive us to public school in a snowstorm when we missed the school bus, and Nana who was there with cookies and milk when we got home. We would talk and Nana would share stories that always subtly ended in a life lesson. Nana had polio as a child, and it left her with scoliosis. When she walked hunched over from her Ford LTD station wagon into the store, I often held her hand. Kids from school would tease me. I said, "It's ok, Nana. They're just jealous they don't have their grandmother's hand to hold." One day, some bully overheard me. They didn't tease me after that. Nana died of cancer during March break of my ninth grade year. I was 13 and a half; she would have been 84 that July. Before she left this earth, she ensured that I'd learned her life lesson: "Love many, trust few, and always paddle your own canoe."

I felt like I was completely alone in the world after Nana died. My parents' marriage, already in trouble before Nana's death, disintegrated. I turned to my dad, my second angel. Despite what he was going through personally, he was my Scout leader, my boat driving instructor, my high school homework coach (even though he never finished ninth grade) and he was involved in my everyday life. Even to this day, he is my rock. Without him, God knows where I'd be today. Dad always took the time to listen to me, to hear me out, to ask questions about what I wanted, and then offer his sound advice: "Never mind the past. Today is the first day of the rest of your life. You can achieve anything you set your mind to, I believe in you son."

By September of my grade 10 year, I was invited to try out for the grade 13 band—the "Wind Ensemble." At my high school, music was as cool as football, and both had many awards hanging in the halls. The band instructor, who wouldn't even know he was an angel to me, was Mr. Douglas Walker. Mr. Walker was an incredibly gifted music educator whose talents were largely under-appreciated as a high school teacher in our small rural town. Mr. Walker maintained that it wasn't about him—it was about the music, and more importantly about the students who made the music. He said the music was already in us—he just helped us express it. His message was "Don't die with your music still inside you," and as he raised his baton, he encouraged us to persist until by saying with a smile "Meet you at the end."

I graduated high school, and within two weeks at university, I found my fourth angel—a hippie race car driving rebel turned marine mechanic and exceptional university professor named Mr. Cam McRae. I applied for a job in the Wilfrid Laurier psych department research lab to earn some money. Cam hired me, and over the next four years that I was lucky enough to be permitted to hang around him for many more hours than I was paid. He taught me how to navigate the politics of an institution, how to achieve what you want ethically, and so much more. Cam listened for hours to all of my life's troubles, and introduced me to freelance writing helping me find what he called "my voice." Initially part-time, my freelance writing career helped pay for school as I got published in our university campus paper, then *Outdoor Canada*, then *The Toronto Star.* I soon expanded my freelance career to full-time as a syndicated eco-journalist, marine website manager, how-to DIY producer for PowerBoat Television, and finally as the editor for *Power Boating Canada* for over a decade now. It was Cam who taught me how to be a counselor, by being mine to this day, and often quoted the aphorism on his office door: "The unexamined life isn't worth living, ah, yes, but the unlived life isn't worth examining!"

My two daughters are my fifth and six angels. Each of their births was a life-changing moment for sure. Unfortunately, when they were just four years and 18 months old, their mom and I split. And so began an incredibly nasty divorce that would last over four years. I fought for my daughters' rights to have both their parents, their mother and their father, in their lives in a meaningful way each day. I spent every penny I had, and many more that I was fortunately able to borrow, and thanks to my LegalShield membership and an awesome lawyer, I eventually won the right to be in my girls' lives half the time. In Ontario, back sixteen years ago, that judgment was almost unheard of. I wanted to be Daddy. I had absolutely no intentions of just paying child support, or being referred to as an "every-other-weekend-Disney-dad." I wanted to be an involved parent who was there to teach my daughters to tie their shoes, to read a book, to write, to learn, to think for themselves, and to achieve good marks. And I wanted to show them how to swim, to downhill ski, to ride a bike, to paddle a boat, and to drive a car so they could head off into their own exciting future at the university of their choice. I wanted to be there to walk them down the aisle someday at their wedding. I'm most proud to be introduced as simply "my Daddy."

At a time when MSN messenger was all the rage, long before texting, Snapchat, Facebook or Instagram, and at a time when I had just about given up near the end of my four year divorce, this woman smiled at me on a dating website (way back when they were in their infancy) the day after Valentine's Day. And so appeared what would turn out to be my seventh angel—Moira, my wife. Divorced herself, after her husband cheated on her while she was pregnant, we two souls were searching—but very, very cautiously. Three weeks of phone calls led to a dinner date that went well, lead to four months of dating without telling our girls (she had her own daughter), and six months of dating with our girls. I proposed that Christmas. I wanted a wife, an equal partner in life, in love, and in business, and I wanted a role model for my daughters. Moira was and is all of the above in amazing abundance.

I was so far in debt that it seemed hopeless to even dream of seeing the light of day. Yet, searching for a way out, I stumbled across a business model and a group of mentors who were willing to pour into my wife and me, to teach us things we didn't know and coach us to be successful in ways I never knew were possible. The timeless wisdom of Jim Rohn's words, the daily coaching of Mike Melia, the friendship of Rob and Charlene Mackenzie, and teaching from so many more have taught us that words matter and thoughts become things. We understood that we were the authors of our own lives. We write our own story by what we do daily. We are where we are today based on our thoughts and actions of yesterday. That took a while to sink in. Once it did, we began to think better and do things differently. We began with the end in mind—freedom and choice—and we worked the slight edge purposely each day to achieve that dream.

The amazing people we have had the opportunity to first meet, and now work with, in our business have collectively been my eighth angel. Sharing with them what we learned, helping them achieve their goals and dreams— one step and one day at a time—while working from home, raising our daughters, and caring for our aging parents, has been so very rewarding to me. Together so far we have impacted over ten thousand individual's lives directly, and many more indirectly, and the promise of what is still to come is so very exciting. We are achieving our goals by helping others achieve theirs—incredible!

So that evening, sitting there in front of our Christmas tree, as I reflected on how infinitely beyond grateful I was for those angels in my life; the real question came to me. How do we give thanks to our angels in a way that appropriately honors the true and lasting impact they have made on us?

The only answer that I've been able to come up with is to actively search for ways to pay it forward and be an angel for someone else who needs one today. I've attempted to do that, in my years of service in Scouting, in raising our daughters, and in coaching the team members we've been so fortunate to be gifted with. Helping others become their best is something I absolutely love doing.

Bundled all together, my life's message is "Say what you mean, mean what you say, just don't be mean when you say it. Live, love, laugh, learn and yes, even cry...and as you depart, ensure that you've given far more than you received."

TWEETABLE

We give thanks to the angels who've helped us by being an angel to someone else. Who needs you to be their angel today?

Brad Roberts earned a masters degree in psychology at a formal university, and his coaching and mentoring degree through experience at the school of life. A father, husband, award-winning journalist, and successful international business owner, his passion is to help others find freedom and to design a life they don't need to escape from each weekend through service to others, entrepreneurship, and actively chasing their dreams. You can reach him at brad@bmroberts.com or toll free at 1 877 323 4965.

CHAPTER 30

The Sounds of Life
by Cornelius Butler

"Imagine you were without sight for a moment and had to rely on your other four senses to interpret life's journey. With your hearing heightened and fully aware, do you like the sounds of life that you are hearing right now? Do you like the voices that are speaking into your life? Do you like the situation that you are in right now? Do you like the opportunities available to you right now? Does the situation feel right?"

– Cornelius Butler

This is what I call the sounds of life. It is the opportunity to interrupt life by evaluating the sounds around you. How would you like to be the featured star in a movie, the movie that we call life? If you accept this invitation, you must be willing to fill the front row, learn, and listen to the soundtrack of the premiere to your life.

I had an unexpected interruption in my life. In the summer of 1987 I had a seizure at my grandmother's house. Here is where the little-known concept I call the sounds of life kicks in. My dad had just got off from work and was on his way home when he heard the roaring sirens of the Richmond Fire Department behind him. He pulled over to let the emergency vehicle past and then proceed on his route. The same left turn that my dad needed to take to get home is the same left turn the fire department took. "Someone in the neighborhood needs help," my dad thought to himself, until the emergency vehicle stopped right in front of the same house my dad was going to.

The situation just got real. As the fire department raced into the house for triage, so did my dad, leaving his car double parked in front of the house with the hazard lights on as if it too was an emergency vehicle. There I was, lying on the floor in my mother's arms, exhausted from the shaking convulsions of a seizure. The paramedics were able to stabilize my vitals and whisk me off to the hospital. The doctors performed a CT scan and delivered the bad news to us in the emergency room that day.

They found something. I had a malformation, an aneurysm in the right side of my brain. I was immediately put on seizure control medicine and was given strict doctors' orders not to do anything strenuous or strain myself mentally or physically. Man, I thought to myself, "Talk about walking on eggshells." My ninth grade year was a year of just: go to school, take medicine, and relax. On top of that, my favorite cousin Chester was murdered, and my parents did not even tell me until a year after he was buried and gone in an attempt to shield me from stress.

My doctor told me that I could continue in physical education, that I could play in the band, and that I could play baseball when the season began. But football was out of the picture because it is such a contact sport. I needed surgery, and it would not be wise to continue to play afterwards. So, there went part of my dream of making a name for myself that school year. I had played football in Richmond for the Richmond Steelers since 1982. My health took away my hopes in football and as for a career in baseball, I just never got that lucky break. It just didn't happen. I played in the Richmond Pony Baseball League since 1979. I could have made a living at playing either one of these sports. I believe that in my heart.

Surgery was the only way to correct this problem, and in the summer of 1988, my pediatrician told me, "Cornelius, two weeks before your surgery I would like you to try something. Now, this is not American Medical Board certified yet, but it's something that we are considering looking at: the power of the mind. Now, two weeks before your surgery I want you to lay in your bed and use your imagination to see the scalpel cutting your head. When you see this, I want you to imagine yourself turning off the blood circulation like you turn off the facets to your water. Cornelius, this is so you don't bleed as much. Then I want you to image yourself healing up just fine with no complications. This is so you heal up quicker."

I remember a poster I had on my wall that said, "Minds are like parachutes they only work when they are open." Me being sixteen and open-minded, I tried my doctor's instructions. Now here comes the sounds of life again. My surgery was only supposed to be a two-week process and the goal was to complete the surgery during the summer, so I would not miss any school, but for some reason, the surgery was postponed, and it seemed like it might not even take place at all. Two weeks before school was to start, I started to hemorrhage in my brain. I walked into my parent's room and laid down on the bed and said, "Mama, I feel hot," and that was it.

My mom knew something wasn't right about this situation and immediately began to pray. My mom's prayer was, "Lord I know you gave your son for the whole world, but if it be your will to take my son, I will let you have him. But if it is not your will to take my son, I would like to keep him around for a little bit." This is where my mom got clarity on the scripture, the "Lord giveth and the Lord taketh away." and "I am come that they might have life, and that they might have it more abundantly."

The next thing I remember is the ambulance ride. I remember going in and out of consciousness. I can still recall the sound of the engine and the closing of the doors. I guess the altered state of consciousness allowed me to hear and see things as needed. Because I was hemorrhaging, this was a life or death situation. Surgery was immediately needed and could not be performed at the hospital I was at. I needed to be transported to the Children's Hospital in Oakland, California. And to top it off, my doctor was on vacation in Hawaii. A call was made to my doctor, and in what seemed to be a life or death panic moment, my doctor saw the opportunity of a lifetime. Because I was hemorrhaging slowly, my doctor ordered the hospital to put something in my IV to make my blood clot. When he returned the very next day, he would know exactly where to go to correct the aneurysm.

The day of my surgery, right outside the surgery doors, I had a sudden realization. A tear rolled down my cheek. Even though my brain surgeon made me feel confident in his ability to perform the procedure, my thought was this: "This is the brain, the control center. What if I can't see when I wake up, or what if I can't remember, or lose my motor skills." My mind started racing with all the what ifs.

What quieted my mind and anxiety was remembering an old gospel song called "Wait on the Lord." I pictured myself sitting outside of heaven's gate sitting on a rock. And I sang that song to myself, "Lord, I going to wait here sitting on this rock until you show up, I don't care how long it takes." The gate opened and all I saw was the bottom of an olive-green robe and sandals. A hand extended to me, and I went walking on the other side of the gate. Because I was so bound by fear, I did not have the attention span to look around and enjoy the scenery. I just remember not even walking, but floating, and I was so afraid to let go that I held on with two hands.

My six hour surgery was a success. My doctor said to me, "Cornelius, we completely removed the aneurysm, so you don't have to come back, and you only bled ten CCs." As he was walking out of the room, I said, "Wait a minute. How much is ten CCs?" He took his pointer finger and thumb and made the letter C, then said, "That is how much ten CCs was." As he walked out of the room, I said to myself "Wow, so it did work." Using my imagination like my pediatrician told me worked.

I was so intrigued by this that I wanted to discover and understand what it was I did by faith that manifested itself physically. My thought process was, if I could do this by faith with my surgery, I could apply this to business and make money at will.

Years later, I remember sharing this story with a friend of mine who said, "You need to get the book called *The Power of the Subconscious Mind* by Dr. Joseph Murphy." This is where my journey of understanding began. With this new found understanding and awareness, I said another prayer because I felt that I was armed and equipped to go out into the business arena and play. But I knew there were several different businesses I could pick from and get into, and with no real-world education or expectation of what I wanted, I knew I could be taken advantage of. My prayer was this: "Lord I made you the Lord of my life, and you brought me through my surgery. Now I would like to make you the Lord of my business so that I never get into the wrong business venture."

I went to the bookstore the very next day and sitting on the shelf was a book titled *Think and Grow Rich*. I looked up to the ceiling and said, "You funny." I immediately purchased the book because scripture says, "So as a man thinketh in his heart so is he."

I said, "If this book is going to teach me how to think rich, then I want my thoughts to be filled with riches." I also bought that day *How to Make It Big in the Seminar Business*. Now, this is where I noticed and was made consciously aware of the sounds of life. I noticed that, whatever you want to do in life, and whatever you are supposed to be doing, it is somehow in some way in your life, and always has been. You just haven't discovered it yet.

For me, I hated reading. I even had my girlfriend at the time, who is now my wife, finish reading my English book in high school to pass the class. She got us an A. But, at age 21, I forced myself to read this book *Think and Grow Rich*. And the more I read it, the more I could not put it down. I understood now why I hated reading. None of the books in school piqued my interest the way personal development books did. In the book *How to Make It Big in the Seminar Business* was a phone number—my first connection closer to the business arena. I dialed the number in the book and Sandy Karn of Wheaton, Illinois answered the phone. We connected. I remember her talking about a business opportunity that held mastermind meetings. I had just read about masterminds in *Think and Grow Rich*. Turns out that book is where they got the concept from! I looked up again and said, "You funny."

Sandy proceeded to tell me that the business opportunity was a success television network that had all motivational speakers come on the show. I thought to myself, "Wow, not only can I read about it, I can now watch it on TV and get paid for it." Personal development attached to a business opportunity has taught me the powerful concept of having mentors speak in your life. I have learned to call my indirect friends, the authors of the books I was reading, my mentors. Through personal development, I was taught early in my twenties to invest in myself. Money was always a barrier for me, and I could not always afford to go to the conferences or afford to pay for the workshops. But I was always hungry and thirsted for the knowledge. That is the reason I stayed in the bookstore and joined the success television network TPN. Over the years I learned that you and anyone else are connected through five degrees of separation. I was in Darren Hardy's downline under Sandy Karn. At the time I had no idea who Darren Hardy was. I also learned that your income will always be in direct ratio (within five thousand dollars) of your five closest friends. I at that time said, "All my friends are in books, so I must be in good company."

My income was nowhere near my new friends' income, but just like when I played baseball in 1979, I realized that I was on a new playing field and that I could not just expect to walk onto any new arena and perform at peak level even though the ambition was brewing inside me. I had to learn from the ones that came before me, and I was so grateful that they were willing to share the knowledge and experience with me either through a book or tape series.

Most average people tend to look at the personal development industry as "those speakers are getting rich off you buying their books." I tell them the same way, "You know that university you are doing? You're paying tuition buying books and learning." I was introduced to another one of my mentors, Jim Rohn, who taught me that there are two types of education. 1. A formal education, which will get you a job. 2. An informal education, which you learn in books, tapes, seminars, and journals, will make you wealthy. That connected with me. Now I understood why I was on the path I was on. What you are willing to do for free in your spare time will greatly multiply itself in your future.

Here is my conclusion after listening to my sounds of life. My adversity altered the course of my previous plan. I recall reading a book by Laura Beth Jones, *Jesus CEO*, and reading the chapter "Don't Kick Your Donkey." My donkey was my aneurysm, which connected me to my pediatrician Dr. Michael Erickson, now retired. This doctor encouraged me to use the power of my own imagination to prepare for my surgery. This led me to connect with brain surgeon Dr. Michael Taekman and Dr. Almakeen. The success of my surgery led me to Dr. Joseph Murphy, author of *The Power of the Subconscious Mind*. A prayer connection to God led me to Napoleon Hill, author of *Think and Grow Rich* through whom I met Sandy Karn in the book *How to Make It Big in the Seminar Business* by Paul Karaski. This led me to the success television network TPN, part of Darren Hardy's organization under the CEOs Jeff Olsen and Eric Worre. Through them, I was introduced to Jim Rohn via an audio tape. I consider every book, every author that has spoken into my life, a friend, a mentor, and part of my mental advisory board, with God sitting at the head of the table. People tell me that I am wise beyond my years, and I humbly say thank you. But I know why and where my wisdom comes from.

TWEETABLE
What you want to and should be doing in life is in your life and always has been. Listen to and interpret the sounds of life to discover it.

Cornelius Butler is founder of Millionaires On Deck Enterprise, a network of like-minded business professionals from all walks of life who started from humble beginnings, and Executive Director Level Independent Associate at LegalShield.

LegalShield provides equal access to the justice system and a gateway to financial freedom through business ownership. For more information on becoming empowered by their legal membership or starting your financial freedom journey, reach out to corneliusbutler@millionairesondeck.com

CHAPTER 31

From Broken to Beautiful
The Art of Gratitude
by Jackie Duty

Chile was under the reign of Augusto Pinochet in the early 1970s when my grandmother fled to the United States. She returned later to get her children, but could only bring the four youngest with her. My mother and her sister were over 18 years old and worked for three years to get their visas so they could come as well. By then, my mother was engaged and in position to live a very comfortable life as she received her family inheritance. She came to this country with an intention to say goodbye to her family here, go back home to Chile, and marry her fiancé. Two weeks before she was going to fly back, she met my dad at a bowling alley in Alton, IL. He convinced her to stay a few more months. He fell in love right away and began proposing marriage.

My father was a good, hard-working man who was trying to build a life as he worked in a steel mill. After a tragic accident that almost took his life, my mother realized how much she had fallen for him. She would walk three miles to the hospital every day to visit him. When he proposed again, she happily accepted. My mother wrote a letter to the family in Chile and chose to let go of a life of luxury and wealth to marry my father. They never had much money, but I have never seen two people so in love. They showed me that love is so much more important than anything else.

I was born a few years later. Born small, I came out fighting at less than five pounds with the umbilical cord wrapped around my throat four times. I was purple, and the doctors said I wouldn't make it. I have had to fight to survive ever since.

I was bullied in school as most kids were, but I learned to pretend like everything was fine. I worked three jobs my senior year of high school to help pay the mortgage because Dad was laid off from the steel mill again.

I dreamed of running away to New York when I turned 19 and pursuing a career in acting. I had visions of being rich and famous. Selfishly, my desires were focused around using wealth to create a lifestyle of extravagance and leisure. I made foolish choices and found myself pregnant at 18, two weeks before my birthday. I didn't know until I was four and a half months along because I continued to lose weight and showed no other signs of being pregnant. I fought the thoughts of abortion. My mom went ballistic and refused to allow me to kill her grandchild. If I didn't want this child, she would raise him herself.

At 3:23 am on my 19th birthday, I woke up in a pool of blood. My mom came running into my room when she heard me scream. She looked devastated, told me I had lost the baby, and rushed me to the emergency room. Doctors surrounded me and were very cold and unsympathetic as they informed me that I lost one child, and I would probably lose the second. I had no idea that I was having twins. They advised me to go home, put my feet up, and let them know when it happened. Later that day, I was getting my first ultrasound. Because I was so far along, they were able to tell that it was a boy, and if he were born, he would be born with Down Syndrome. Nothing happened. I was still pregnant.

In a state of shock and not knowing what to do, I traveled to the park that I grew up with. This was my place of solitude where I would go to be alone and contemplate life's circumstances. I sat alone, under a tree by a lake, as I attempted to process everything. As I sat there, I could only think about a childhood friend that had drowned in that lake several years earlier. So many emotions began to overwhelm me as I thought about what an incredible young woman she would have been if she didn't die at such an early age. Why did she die? Why did God choose her instead of me? All I could think about was the poor choices I had made. Hopelessness surrounded me, and I almost did something very stupid that day that would have devastated my family. I am so thankful that God showed up in a very big way. He told me to pick up my mat and walk. I have a purpose. My son has a purpose. We will walk together. I stood up and made a decision to keep moving forward and never give up.

Later that week, I found myself back in church after spending so many years running away from God. Sweet, little old ladies prayed for the health of my unborn child. A few days later, I was visiting specialists in a hospital in St. Louis. As I was getting my next ultrasound, one doctor walked in, read the scan, and didn't say a word. He left and sent three more doctors to look at the results. Then they left and didn't come back for 30 minutes. It was the longest 30 minutes of my life as I wondered and contemplated the cause of their strange behavior. They finally returned and said they couldn't explain it, but this baby was perfectly healthy and showed no signs of Down Syndrome as previously diagnosed.

Tyler was born in March of 2001. He was and has continued to be one of the healthiest children and a true blessing to our family.

This began a journey of me trying to figure out my purpose beyond my selfish desires of fame and fortune. I was no longer living for me, but for my child. Tyler's father, Steve, and I were married a few months later. Then I found a new, great-paying job making $8 an hour at a local newspaper in the advertising department. This was a huge increase. I started at $4.15 an hour working several jobs, working my way up to $6 an hour flipping pizzas. To have the luxury of sitting in an office making $8 an hour with no college degree, I thought I hit the jackpot.

At 23, I began to have success in the business world. I became very arrogant, even vowing that I wouldn't be like my parents and file bankruptcy and lose our house. I declared that I would make my first million by the time I was 30. I focused on building wealth and started to realize success. I also started to pray for another child. I would dream about my daughter.

At age 24, I found out I was pregnant again. I was overjoyed and couldn't wait to tell Steve. I never got the chance to tell him. Steve and I had a huge fight, so I never told him before I miscarried my daughter. I couldn't have been more than 8 to 10 weeks pregnant. I was broken as I held, what science would call a fetus, but who I knew was the daughter I would never see grow up. I buried her quietly and never spoke of it until a year ago. I got stuck in a great depression until I buried myself in work to numb the pain.

I was so excited when I found out we were having my second son, Trevor. He brought so much joy back into my life, and I refocused on hitting the goals that I set. I closed on my first rental property on my 26th birthday. I made the classic mistake that everyone else made in 2008. I overextended and made many foolish choices. This launched a series of events that you could call a perfect storm. I did everything I said I would never do. I filed bankruptcy and lost two houses.

Steve and I worked to rebuild everything we lost. We were starting to see the light at the end of the tunnel, when I lost my job. Two weeks later, Steve lost his job. We had no insurance and no way to pay our bills. We were in a complete faith walk knowing that God is provision, not our jobs.

In July of that year, my son's friend Gregory died from HLH. He was 13 and the most incredible kid I have ever met. He was the oldest of five children and had a heart of gold. I prayed over him for five hours the day he died. I left the hospital with hope and conviction that he would survive. I received a text a few hours after I got home that he had passed away.

This broke me. On the ministry team, we had been praying for people and seeing miracles every week. People were getting healed of cancer, glaucoma, chronic back pain, and much more. Crazy miracles were happening every week. Gregory was my pastor's son. I couldn't fathom the thought that Gregory would not also receive his miracle. He HAD to be ok. When he died, I was devastated.

The next day, I was trying to control the chaos in my life, so naturally, I went to my garage and started to organize and clean shelves. This was my coping mechanism to gain control at a time when I felt completely helpless. I fell off a ladder and broke both legs. My left heel broke in three places. My right ankle was so severely sprained, I couldn't walk on it. Without insurance I couldn't even afford a wheelchair. It is so humbling to have to beg someone to borrow a wheelchair because you can't afford one.

That summer, God worked a miracle: my husband and I fell in love. I learned that I never really loved him because I never really loved myself. It was too painful to be that vulnerable. This became the summer I let go of my pride and allowed myself to really see Steve as God sees him. He is a good man, and for the first time in our 13-year marriage, we were focused on one vision and moving in the same direction. We didn't have much, but we had our family and hope for a better tomorrow. That was all we needed to keep moving forward. We started to rebuild. A few years later, after more success in corporate media, I started and sold my first marketing agency. I felt this was a pivotal moment of regaining and re-establishing myself in the business world.

In December 2016, I accepted a new, exciting position at Fox 2 News in St. Louis. The company and people were incredible. I was very excited about the direction we were moving. Six days after I started this new career, I received a phone call at work. I could barely understand my mom as she cried that my house had just burned to the ground.

In one day, everything I owned crumbled to ashes. Not knowing where to go and having nothing but literally one car and the clothes on our backs, I turned to friends and family for help. The following day, I was on my way to meet my friend, Stacey, who was going to help me get some clothes and figure out my bills. As I was driving to meet her, my car and last material possession, broke down on the highway. Stacey picked me up, and we could only laugh at the insanity of the situation. Sometimes all you can do is laugh. She helped me through one of the toughest days of my life.

Everything that Steve and I were trying to rebuild was gone. In one day, we lost everything. All we had left were the clothes on our back. They weren't even my favorite clothes, because it was laundry day and I was way behind on the laundry. In the weeks that followed, I was unprepared for the emotions that developed from the realization that everything from my childhood, my husband's childhood, and my children's childhoods was gone. Every keepsake that we had cherished, that represented our lives, was gone forever. Pictures that can never be replaced, family heirlooms...all gone.

I went back to the park and sat under my tree. I stared at the water rolling calmly as I shivered in the cold. I was numb for a moment. Then I remembered the day, sixteen years prior, when I found my purpose. It was never about me. A renewed clarity emerged as I stood up. As long as I wake up every morning with breath in my lungs, I have a new opportunity to have an impact. Every person has a story to tell. Every person has moments of impact throughout life. It is what you choose to do after that moment of impact that will define your tomorrows.

I am so thankful to have been so blessed in life. I am surrounded by amazing people who are impacting lives every day. My heart burns to help people discover their purpose. If you are alive today, you have beaten the odds and have an incredible purpose that is waiting to be fulfilled. Many have told me that they have been through too much or are too "broken." My response is "Use it." Without sacrifice there is no value. Use your brokenness as a catalyst to launch you into your destiny.

Kintsugi is the Japanese art of repairing broken pottery with lacquer dusted or mixed with gold. This demonstrates how they highlight the cracks and broken places as simply an event in the life of the object that built its character rather than allowing its service to end at the time of the damage or breakage. The brokenness is highlighted, not discarded.

My life has been a demonstration of how the master potter can take a broken mess and make something arguably even more beautiful. If we are vulnerable enough to highlight the broken places in our life, God can demonstrate His love for you. Your life can then be used to deliver hope to others that can be going through a breaking process in their lives.

As my story continues to unfold, I am determined to use my experiences to create purpose that fulfills my desire to give to others in times of desperation and need. What is my "one thing" that changed everything? It's not one thing. It has been a series of "things" that led to a pivotal moment where my perspective changed. In choosing to not be a victim, I made a choice to live with purpose beyond circumstances that can create pain or hopelessness. I made a choice to live as a Deliverer of Hope. I don't know what your current circumstance is, but I know you have a choice on how you move forward. Don't be afraid to take risks and pursue your passion. Turn your fear into fire. When the fire inside of you burns greater than the fires around you, you are positioned to pursue your life's purpose and deliver hope. Let's run and be relentless in the pursuit of purpose.

TWEETABLE

Let the fire inside of you burn greater than the fires around you. Restore brokenness and honor the journey. #FireWithin #NeverGiveUp #ArtOfGratitude

Jackie Duty owns an event company while growing a global mobile company. She is a life coach and works as the Chief Development Director at an international prep school. Prior to that, she spent 16 years helping hundreds of businesses in corporate media. She led marketing sales departments in newspapers, 11 radio stations, TV, magazines and developmental digital platforms. She successfully executed over 300 events with up to 20,000+ people. To have her speak at your event, visit her website at jackieduty.com

CHAPTER 32

The Greatest Lesson I Ever Learned

by Marco Santarelli

My parents immigrated from Italy and were very humble people. My dad was a machinist and my mother worked two jobs to help us stay ahead. We were not wealthy. But from an early age, I knew there were wealthy people all around. You couldn't always identify them by how they dressed or what car they drove, but I knew I wanted to be financially free (i.e., "rich").

At 13 years old, I couldn't drive, but I would get my father to take me down to the computer store to buy software for my old Radio Shack TRS-80 computer. That's when I bought a book to teach myself assembly language and started coding a new game. The idea was to have fun but also to sell this game. With only 4K (a minuscule 4 kilobytes) of memory, you run out of memory very quickly. I couldn't finish coding my game, but it was a great learning experience, and I knew then I was an entrepreneur of some kind.

I later met a man who was a hospital janitor. He was one of the last people you'd think would have a portfolio of rental properties. He and his wife would save up, buy a property, then save up and buy a property again. I don't know if they were financially free, but they were doing very well. This "wealthy" janitor convinced me that real estate was the direction I needed to go.

When I finally turned 18, I jumped in and purchased my first rental property. I had to wait until I was 18 because I couldn't qualify for financing until then. I purchased an end-unit townhome, stripped it down, and renovated it with the help of my uncle who was a carpenter. There was no internet back then, so I had to put a sign out on the lawn to attract potential tenants.

The whole experience was textbook. I never took a course or attended a workshop. It just felt right.

PERSONAL DEVELOPMENT

I'm a big believer in personal development. You probably are too because you're reading this book. In my early twenties, I enjoyed building radio-controlled model airplanes. While I worked, in the background I would always play personal development cassette tapes—remember those? I still have the original Anthony Robbins Personal Power cassettes. That Tony Robbins course was one of the first personal development programs that I ever bought. I still have it today because it had such an impact on me. But that wasn't the only one. I was also listening to Jim Rohn, Brian Tracy, and many others. I've always loved that stuff.

I started early on my entrepreneurial path, but like everyone else, I did not follow a straight line. There were many hurdles and roadblocks on my journey. However, I see obstacles like the bumpers in a pinball machine. You have to bounce your way forward towards your destination. Your journey will rarely be a straight line. You need to take action and be tenacious in getting where you want to go.

MY DOTCOM DREAM GONE BUST

I moved to California in 1998 during the dotcom boom to start a new business with my cousin, a publisher in the private/country club industry. We created a spin-off company in the dotcom space. It was a Costco.com type of business that we called eClubBuy. We referred to the business as the place where clubs could order everything from toilet paper to tractors. We raised $9.5 million in venture capital and ultimately hired over 100 employees. I was the third co-founder and CTO with the largest department in the company. Not too shabby for a 30-year old.

Ultimately, this turned out to be a bad thing when on March 13th, 2000 the NASDAQ crashed. Like most other dotcom businesses, we were not cash flow positive and could not sustain ourselves. Our venture capital funding dried up, and we had to start laying people off. Our company had a burn-rate of over $100,000 a month, and you can only last for so long when you're blowing through that kind of cash. In the end, I was the third last person to leave before closing the doors forever.

It's pretty cool when you're on a fast-track like that, with all those stock options, thinking about the day your company goes public in an IPO and you become an "overnight" multi-millionaire. We were on our way towards a pre-IPO, but sadly that never happened.

The last thing I wanted to do at that time was get back into corporate America. So, I ended up taking some time off. I had the fortunate luxury of being able to do that.

I had to ask myself, "What do I really enjoy?" I loved real estate, I loved investing, and I didn't know it at the time, but I loved helping people.

Then in mid-2003, I got this mysterious email from a guy named Robert G. Allen. He authored many books, many with Mark Victor Hansen, and is known as one of the grandfathers of "nothing down" real estate investing. His email was an invitation to a free three-day real estate investing workshop in Orange, CA. Since I loved real estate and wasn't working, I obviously decided to go.

The event was outstanding. The speaker, Glenn Purdy, was so entertaining and so engaging, that nobody got up to go to the toilet while he was on stage. At the end of the day, it was amazing to see how many people went to the back of the room with credit cards in hand to sign up for their real estate boot camps. I too whipped out my credit card and signed up for their program which started at $15,000 and ran up to $35,000 (excluding travel, hotel, food, etc.).

THE LIGHTBULB MOMENT
As I attended those boot camps, I quickly realized that I already knew most of what they were talking about. But it was fun for me to be there because I got to network with like-minded people. I started buying a lot of property very quickly. In less than two years I had acquired 84 rental units. And people started coming to me with questions.

They were asking:

Where are you finding these properties?

How are you negotiating them?

How are you structuring the deal?

Can you coach me?

Can you find me some good properties too?

And that's when the lightbulb moment happened for me. There was an opportunity for me to help other people, show them what I was doing, and give them an opportunity to be successful doing the same thing I was doing—investing in rental real estate.

Even though people were going through the same boot camps as I was, I found they were getting some education but still couldn't pull the trigger. I could "take them by the hand" and walk them through the same process I was using. And that's how my business, Norada Real Estate Investments, was born in January 2004.

Today we help investors purchase over 400 properties a year. They're people from all walks of life who want to acquire completely turn-key single-family homes, duplexes, and fourplexes. These are properties that are tenant-occupied, professionally managed, cash-flow positive, and in good neighborhoods within good markets around the United States.

Our core business is helping people build their real estate portfolios so that they can create wealth and passive income as hassle-free as possible. We choose to be completely agnostic, which means we are not married to any market, neighborhood, property manager, rehabber, inspector, title company, or anything like that.

The United States has over 400 MSAs (metropolitan statistical areas), so it's a very big country. Each market is unique. Being agnostic allows us to be nimble and properly serve our investor's needs to accomplish their financial goals.

THEN CAME THE PODCAST

In June 2015 I started a podcast called Passive Real Estate Investing as a way to provide free education and continue to give back to people looking for help. Since then I've had many great guests including Rich Dad Advisor Tom Wheelwright, Rich Dad Advisor Ken McElroy, as well as asset protection and syndication attorney Mauricio Rauld. I'm humbled to say it often ranks in the top three most popular real estate podcasts.

On my show, I often share my 10 Rules of Successful Real Estate Investing. My first rule of successful real estate investing is to educate yourself. Contrary to popular belief that ignorance is bliss, *ignorance is expensive*. The more you learn the more you earn. The more you understand about investing and finance, the better an investor you will become. You will understand the difference between a bad, a good, and a great deal. You'll understand when you're being sold something that doesn't pass the "smell test."

We don't get real financial education in school. We barely learn how to balance a checkbook. That's one of the reasons my wife and I homeschool our daughter.

It is so easy to educate yourself today with the amount of content that is out there. Books, podcasts, live events, even Google are powerful resources. Knowledge is a currency. Everything starts with what you know. If you don't know something, you need to find out. The more you know, the better off you will be.

You know the saying that knowledge is power? Well, that's only a half-truth. Knowledge gives you the ability to see opportunities so that you can take the right action. The reality is, *applied* knowledge is power. I have found that to be true my whole life!

I'm not different or special, I just saw an opportunity at the right time and took action. Action is everything. Action is the game changer. You can wish all you want. You can want something really bad, and think about it all the time, but until the "rubber meets the road" nothing will happen. You need to push yourself to achieve what you desire.

Educate yourself, identify opportunities, and take action today!

TWEETABLE
Educate yourself, identify opportunities, and take action today!

Marco Santarelli is an investor, author and the founder of Norada Real Estate Investments – a nationwide provider of turnkey cash-flow rental properties. Since 2004, they've helped over 1,000 real estate investors create wealth and passive income through real estate. He's also the host of the Passive Real Estate Investing *podcast.*

Listen and learn about real estate investing at PassiveRealEstateInvesting.com

CHAPTER 33

How I Live by "If You Don't Like Your Outcomes, Change Your Responses!"

By Jon Gorosh

I've lived an interesting life and I've gained a lot of wisdom. Looking back, it's not one tapestry, and there's not one moment that stands out above the others. It's more like a patchwork quilt of moments and their lessons that create who I am today and the wonderful life that I am living. All I can do is give you a glimpse at the many moments of optimism that have shaped the man I am today.

My father was a salesman who won several awards for customer service and accumulated a nice collection of handmade gifts given to him by satisfied clients. He worked 365 days a year to put food on the table. By the bank statement we were not rich, but it was a happy childhood. Even before I read the famous quote by Zig Ziglar, "You can have everything in life you want if you will just help enough other people get what they want," both of my parents showed me by example the importance of volunteering and giving back to the community. I have held that lesson to this day and I am proud to have passed this legacy to both of my daughters.

My family did not eat out often, but when we did, I always made a friendly agreement with my mom: I was allowed to be adventurous by ordering something on the menu I had never tried previously, but I could always switch plates with her if I did not like what I ordered. Turns out, I never wanted to switch plates. To this day I still intentionally order dishes I have never tried while rarely regretting what is on the plate. This was my mother's lesson to get me out of my comfort zone.

Just one week before my 18th birthday and three weeks before I left for Western Michigan University, my father died suddenly from complications of diabetes. Relatives from my father's side came to the funeral, and we spoke for the first time in years. Because of an ongoing argument between my father and his siblings, I grew up not knowing my cousins though they lived a mere few miles away. It was wonderful to see them. I still play with the backgammon set my cousins gave me during the Shiva memorial service at my home. From our reunion, I learned to treat others with respect as you would like to be treated. It is impossible to feel bad and think positive at the same time.

I spent my final semester at Western Michigan as an unpaid intern for my local US Congressman James Blanchard. My responsibility was to communicate with the constituents as a conduit between them and various branches of the local, state, and national government agencies. I witnessed the positive feedback when Mr. Blanchard would remember every constituent's name in every conversation. To see firsthand how our government handles fiduciary responsibilities to accomplish positive change has left me with a lifelong respect for what is possible.

I graduated from Western Michigan University in 1980. Since I was one of many who could not find a decent job in the Detroit area, I knew I had to do something different. By 1981, the local bookstore had a long line out their door every Sunday morning to purchase the *Houston Chronicle* for their classified ads for employment. Their classified ads had more pages than the entire local *Detroit Free Press* newspaper. On Memorial Day weekend in 1981, I joined the caravan from Michigan relocating to Houston. That morning I turned on my car's rear defroster to melt the ice as I left Michigan. At 9:00 pm the same day, I arrived in Little Rock, Arkansas where the outside temperature was still 90 degrees. That was how this Yankee was welcomed to the South.

As I was driving into Houston for the very first time, I paid attention to the billboards to get a feel for the city. There is one billboard in particular I will never forget. In bold letters, it said, "I am proud to be a KiKKer." My first thought was the local Klan had billboards. Imagine my shock. I kept staring. Then I realized each "K" was in the shape of a cowboy boot promoting the local country western radio station. First impressions are not always correct.

The move to Houston was a decision I have never regretted. I had to navigate the numerous twists and turns my career has taken rather than the straight path to financial freedom I desired. Upon my arrival to Houston, when I received an offer in the mail for a credit card, I did not think twice about applying. Unbeknownst to me, someone was opening my apartment mailbox. A thief took a renewal credit card before mine expired later that month. It did not take them long to purchase thousands of dollars of goods. Thank goodness, my credit card company called me since these purchases did not fit my spending pattern due to my parents' legacy not to go into debt to purchase a "want." To recover from my identity theft, I whittled 31 credit cards down to just four major cards and have not had similar issues since.

My education to that point trained me to qualify for a job but not how to survive financially.

For 12 years I was a paralegal. That opportunity originated as a lead from the Job Search Networking Club which I created. While working as a paralegal, a co-worker explained how to become a certified notary signing agent. Over the past few years, I have completed over 2,000 notary assignments. This taught me that education pays dividends sooner or later and to always be open to thinking outside the box.

In 2007, my local bank contacted me about a check that seemed to be forged. Someone had "washed" one of my checks to fraudulently withdraw funds from my checking account. I now pay all my bills online and no longer use personal checks. Around this same time, I noticed a bag of my garbage that I had put by the curb was missing by the time the garbage truck came by the house. Now I shred all documents and mail that has my name on it to avoid any privileged information being left on the curb. My heavy duty crosscut shredder turns paper into confetti and not into long strips that could be reconfigured into a readable document. Once emails were a part of my everyday life, it did not take long for me to realize that some of my received spam showed my personal email address as the sender. To combat hijacking of my email address, I now regularly sweep my laptop for viruses, malware, cookies, and utilize a Virtual Private Network (VPN) to hide my IP address. I also back up my files anticipating when the hard drive eventually crashes, use multiple email addresses to separate business from junk emails, and regularly install vital software updates. These preventative steps have resulted in no more friends of mine receiving spam with my email address as the sender. My financial survival techniques finally emerged.

For the past several years, I have trained to be a private lender under my mentor George Antone. George Antone has written three bestselling books about private lending and personal finance. Survival for a private lender is to borrow money at a rate lower than you loan it back out in a low-risk environment. Be your own bank by controlling and not owing. On the first day of training, George made a side comment about utilizing business lines of credit. If one can accumulate $10,000,000 line of credit and maintain velocity by having these funds always working, the monthly interest earned should be about $100,000. Talk about having an "aha" moment! Everything I had studied, networked, and worked towards all became crystal clear. No one implied it is easy to accumulate a $10,000,000 line of credit, but now I have a goal and a game plan.

It is important to be surrounded by a good team to cover your weaknesses. My whole life I have been described as a jack of all trades and ace of none. Honestly, that fits me pretty well. I hired an attorney to professionally create my corporate entities and to prepare my tax returns. I then signed with companies to analyze my credit bureau reports to improve my FICO® lending profile in preparation for acquiring business lines of credit. It is so important to learn how to properly and efficiently request the credit bureaus remove inaccurate or old information to achieve just one spelling of your name, one address location, and one employer. Achieving this task will reap you many long-term benefits with higher FICO® scores, faster approval of credit, and higher credit limit offers from financial institutions without you having to ask for them. I was taught the value of having the appropriate type of credit cards, the value of having these cards for a long time by avoiding new credit cards (which reduces the overall average length of all cards being open), and the value of having the appropriate carryover monthly balance.

Additional steps I have taken to raise business lines of credit include transitioning my retirement accounts to be self-directed. Only 3-5% of all IRA assets are self-directed even though, according to IRS rules, there are very few prohibited transactions. Established lending guidelines keep risks low and secure when utilizing my self-directed retirement accounts and other people's money (OPM). My personal dividend-paying whole life insurance policy allows me to borrow the cash value as another source for private lending.

Since childhood, I have constantly read biographies, autobiographies, and non-fiction books. Shortly after moving to Houston, I trained at Success Motivation Institute by Paul J Meyer. They emphasized goals must be clearly defined to be achieved. Training with T. Harv Eker taught me that the rich think differently than the poor so I should think like the rich. Thomas J. Stanley wrote a fantastic book emphasizing that your next door neighbor could be a millionaire but you may never realize it based on their appearance and possessions. Wealth is what you accumulate and not what you spend. Advanced training with George Antone opened my eyes that debt can help you achieve financial goals faster, but can also destroy you if not used properly. Finally, my education has taught me how to survive financially.

My path has not been a straight line. But each turn has brought wisdom that has contributed to my success today. Pay attention to the stories in your life. What can you learn from them? What can you use to build your dreams, to better yourself, and to always help others?

TWEETABLE

Obstacles are opportunities in disguise. Focus on your goal and your AHA moment will lead you. Luck is when preparation meets opportunity.

Jon Gorosh uses business lines of credit for low-risk private lending. Identity preservation and raising capital are passions. Jon studied five foreign languages to learn their culture and to comfortably speak with those from any background. Jon treats obstacles as opportunities and credits his daughters Nancy and Stephanie Gorosh and girlfriend Pam Friedman for his positivity. Contact at 713-817-9448 or jon@pdcaprivatelending.com, on Facebook or LinkedIn to talk more.

CHAPTER 34

Getting Found by Getting Lost
How I Crashed a Career to Cash-In on a Life
by Aran Dunlop

"Be yourself; everyone else is already taken."
— Oscar Wilde

Reconciling that my chapter belonged in this book was difficult. Ultimately it was Kyle—whose gift for knowing people better than they know themselves is without equal—who convinced me that it made sense. I've learned to run with his gut on these things.

Rather than leave you with a pithy revelation on the last page, let's get that and all the cornball stereotypes over and done with now. So, "g'day." My name is Aran. This is the story of how I went from a farm kid in New Zealand, to a washed up day trader in Malaysia, to an investment banker, to a self-made real estate millionaire in Miami, making two fortunes, losing them both, and making it all back a few times over along the way.

If I've learned one thing that I can pass along, it's this: your life's mission is to *get to know yourself.* Obviously, not a new concept, yet why do so many of us struggle to internalize it? To explain how I ultimately did, I need to introduce you to a little farm on Te Tahi Rd. It's in rural New Zealand, about five miles outside a "thriving metropolis" of 800 people where I grew up.

It was with all the consternation a five-year-old could process that I received the news that my parents were uprooting and moving us to the big smoke: Melbourne, Australia.

Melbourne was a challenge. Being a Kiwi country kid a year younger than everyone else in the class made for easy prey, and it was a bumpy ride. I figured out how to fit in by the time I finished high school, then moved out when I was 17 to go to college and try on this "new me" in a fresh arena.

Uni was great. I got a job working the register at Kmart and honed my beer drinking talents. After four years I was very ready for it to be over. A part of me was exhausted from the hard work of constantly playing the person I thought others wanted me to be. My flight to Malaysia was in the air hours after my final exam. I didn't even care if I'd passed. I wanted to travel. And, let's be honest—I was 21. I wanted to get laid.

During university, I'd managed to parlay my savings from working at Kmart into a stake of around $20,000 by day trading penny stocks in Australian mining companies. The China boom was just kicking off, and the bull market in Australian stocks made everyone a genius. At the time I thought it was all my brilliance.

With my $20,000 I was able to live in four countries across Southeast Asia for two years while continuing to day trade. Bear in mind; it was 2003. WiFi was new, and working location-free from a laptop in Starbucks was still actually trendy. Doing it from a foreign country was seriously bleeding edge. Sorry to all the newly self-styled millennial "digital nomads." I was doing it before it was cool, four years before the first iPhone was released. Around this "coolness" I constructed a fresh new identity that even I began to believe.

It suddenly stopped feeling cool when I lost all the money. It wasn't a conspiracy, an "unforeseeable market event," or even a careless mistake. It was the law of averages catching up with a lucky fool. Having a hot streak doesn't make you a professional poker player, but that's exactly what I'd thought I was. It hurts when you realize your proudest accomplishments were nothing but luck.

Even worse, I had also lost a further $20,000 borrowed from my parents and friends to trade on their behalf. I was now broke, in a foreign country, desperately clinging to this persona I'd cultivated as a swashbuckling international man of mystery; to myself as much as others.

It *shattered my self-image*. It would happen again, more than once, but the first time I lost my fortune hurt the most. It was disorientating and devastating.

The phrase "finding yourself" has today become such a platitude that it's almost devoid of meaning. Honestly, it's a little nauseating to hear aloud. *Be yourself, Find your inner truth, Follow your passion.*

Bullshit.

I call bullshit because these are not good prescriptions for happiness or success (however you define it). They encourage a pattern of thought that makes us feel that we need to know our passion, our purpose, and who we are, right now. Anxiety emerges when we are unable to nail these answers down in the face of so many others who have apparently succeeded in doing so. Technology and social media feed into these doubts, as Facebook itself has recently admitted. (Their prescription, of course, is more Facebook.)

How do all these people seem to have themselves so together and be living such incredible lives? The voice in our head chimes in: "They're all successful, they're happy, they did it by being themselves and following their passion, and everyone loves them for it.... I must therefore find/be myself/voice/message/brand and follow my passion."

And that is where we fall into the trap of *self-image actualization*—the costly, ruinous shadow version of true self-actualization.

I guaranteed I'd pay back my debts in full, with interest, and within two years I did. The question haunting me the entire time was the creeping dread of: "If I'm not the guy I told myself I was, who on Earth am I?"

There were also more immediate issues. Rent was due, and I was running dangerously low on beer and ramen.

I don't believe in fate, but spookily enough, within two weeks of busting out, I met someone who introduced me to a bond trader at a major Singapore-based investment bank. He told me to "come in tomorrow around lunch." It was 6 pm, the bus ride was six hours, and I didn't have a shirt, dress trousers, or decent shoes, let alone a tie. I completely forgot to bring socks.

To this day I don't know how I got the job. I didn't know what a bond was, and I must've looked like death warmed up after the overnight bus.

I made reasonable money in my first year, more in the second, and an ungodly amount in the third. As I've since found to be the pattern, the more money I made, the more the learning curve flattened, and the further disenchanted I became.

There was a bigger problem. The scar of my prior experience losing everything hadn't healed. I no longer felt safe when things were going well. The experience of having everything pulled out from under you while you're feeling safe and confident never leaves you. I knew, even as I cashed a bonus bigger than every penny I'd earned in my life combined prior, that it would never be enough. *No amount of money alone would ever again make me secure in myself.*

Terrified I'd never again see an opportunity like that job and would regret the decision forever, I quit in February 2009. The amount of money I walked away with felt astronomical to a 27-year-old farm kid. After taxes, I had more than $750,000 in cash. It sounded like enough to retire on at first, but I still had 50-60 years left in me! The fact that interest rates had just dropped to zero didn't help the math. A new dread crept in. I needed to start earning an income again, and I didn't know how to do it.

I'd learned two critical things about myself while working in what was hopefully my last job. The first was that I didn't like working for other people. Not in a virtuous "I'm an entrepreneur and a visionary" way, but in a way that is truly a character flaw. I rebelled against accountability or anything that felt like a boundary on my autonomy. Lunch being at noon was something of an affront. Lunch should be, I thought, whenever I felt hungry. In that regard, there is perhaps a more than a little millennial in me.

The second thing I learned was that if I wanted to live purely from the returns on my investments, I needed to become an outstanding investor. Not solid, not great—outstanding. I needed to make double-digit returns consistently while shielding my downside from catastrophic loss, optimizing my tax strategy, and protecting my assets from public and private predators.

When you've got a steady income, you can safely bat singles and do well investing. With no income, however, my cash was working four jobs: It was my operating capital, my investment capital, my savings, and my rent money. I needed to hit home runs, but I needed to hit home runs without striking out. There was no room for error.

After returning to Australia, I realized I couldn't hit home runs in my own country. Housing prices were still at bubble levels, and regulations were not friendly to small business (and the taxes are a nightmare.) I cast my gaze once more abroad, and they landed on the States. It was here in the US, in 2009, where I found my home runs.

I also discovered I didn't know how to play baseball.

Despite my determination to be a world-class investor, the truth was harsher—I couldn't swing a bat to save myself. Knowing little about the asset class I was working with, the jurisdiction I was dealing in, or the difference between the jungle of private sector business and the comparatively civilized and regulated world of investment banking, I was pummeled. I missed issues with due diligence, allowed tenants to take advantage, suffered theft at the hands of employees, had contractors running rings around me...I could go on.

Sparing the gruesome details, over two years I lost nearly all my money, again. It's embarrassing to even think about today. You could toss a brick out the window and hit a good deal back then. It was a market where it practically took talent to lose money as a buyer. I simply didn't know what

I didn't know, and I wasn't wise enough to test the waters cheaply before risking real capital. I lost hundreds of thousands of dollars making mistakes and learning lessons I could have learned for a fraction of the amount had I known what I know now.

It was déjà vu. I'd burned through a small fortune and was staring at two remaining months of runway before I'd be packing my bags and finding a couch to crash on back in Australia. Something was different though… It didn't affect me emotionally in the way it had seven years earlier, despite dollar losses of 10-20 times the magnitude.

I wasn't afraid of being exposed as a fraud. I was consciously incompetent, while earlier I'd been unconsciously incompetent. There were some sleepless nights, but there was also a sense that in success or failure, the process that lead to the outcome aligned with who I was. If I busted out now, it was only an event. That possibility didn't threaten my sense of self.

As it happened, a lucky turn of events and the intervention of two mentors (to whom I will be forever indebted) arrested the nosedive, and the plane leveled, corrected, and began to climb again from what felt like 10 feet from impact. As I rebuilt my business, that sense of inner security independent of my external appearance of success or failure further matured.

Seven years later as I write this, on a flight from Dubai to Georgia (the country), I feel more aligned with my real self than ever before. I sleep well now knowing that I make decisions striving to be the best version of what I already am rather than trying to be what I think the world wants me to be.

It is on that point I end on what may sound an off-key note. I don't have a mailing list. I don't have a tribe. I don't brand myself. In fact, in being true to myself, I am retreating from all efforts at marketing or promoting myself or my business. What little social media presence I ever had is being carefully dismantled, and any public speaking or promotional work I do is unpaid and in service. Investors or partners I meet through chance encounter or referral.

What do I actually do? Financially, I invest in real estate and businesses around the world. At a deeper level, I discover problems and fault lines. There's usually someone better qualified to fix the problems, truthfully. Often, once the problem is defined, the solution becomes self-evident. I am an opportunity seeker and diagnostician in the broadest sense of the term. I do not have a marketing message or elevator pitch to define it past that, and truthfully I don't feel the need to.

I work with people I like, people I see potential in, people I can learn from, and nothing less. I don't charge for it. In some cases, it becomes organically beneficial to both sides. In others, I am simply grateful to have made a difference and ask only that it be paid forward.

This is my honest, raw, true self. It's not how I've branded, positioned, constructed, or consciously framed myself. It's not optimized, there's no SEO or psychographic voodoo that went into it, and you won't find any selfies trying to paint a picture of it. It's who I permitted myself to be after shedding the masks and layers of what I thought I should have been.

I didn't steal it. It wasn't given to me. I earned it.

If you're feeling stuck, if you have an itch you can't quite scratch, maybe I can help. It might be financial. It might be personal. It might just be something in my story that rings a bell you already feel to be true, but you need a second voice to tell you that you're not crazy.

Or maybe I can't help, who knows. If you want to ask, please reach out to Kyle for my contact information. (Thanks, brother!)

TWEETABLE
I am who I allowed myself to be after shedding the layers of what I thought I should have been.

Aran Dunlop is a Kiwi/Australian self-identifying citizen of the world who runs a private investment firm managing assets for his own portfolio and those of his joint venture partners. His background is international, covering institutional finance, and equity and bond trading, as well as 8 years personally acquiring, developing, and managing multiple classes of commercial real estate with a value exceeding $100 million and private investments in several startup companies. Semi-retired, he spends his time traveling while seeking exceptional new investment opportunities and like-minded people with whom to share them.

CHAPTER 35

The Girl Who Put Her Clothes Back On

by Alicia Lowry

I remember it so clearly. It seems to be many years ago, but in reality, it wasn't long ago. It was pretty simple, really. I would change into outfits and slowly take that outfit off a piece at a time, posing as I did so, resulting in perhaps a few hundred pictures for a new photo set for my website. I found myself in many different locations: professional studios and outdoors spots tucked away barely out of sight. Sometimes we were completely out in the open, not caring about who saw. We shot in Missouri, Las Vegas, California, Hawaii, all over the U.S. I always told myself I had personal limits that many girls who modeled like this did not. This was true, but my limits did not make me feel clean as new. Inside I was angling to retain some needed self-respect.

My career began at one of the most pivotal moments in my life when my family moved to Florida. When I was fourteen, we left behind the small Midwestern town that gave me morals and perspectives that I would not appreciate until I grew older. I will always hold that town and the people there close to my heart, but I am so grateful that we moved away. I can only imagine the person I would have become had we stayed there. My family was a bit dysfunctional, and I was simply a product of them not knowing any better. Life as a child was often difficult for me, but it was also amazing— filled with great friends and a family that loved me.

I was wild because it was what I knew. I found myself interested in boys at a very young age and encouraging my friends to do the same. I always had a strong personality and found myself leading others around me, and unfortunately, I wasn't leading in the best direction. I look back now at some very crazy times and think, "I was a little hard to handle. Compared to my friends, I was the one pushing the envelope."

My girlfriends and I had dreams of becoming models, as many little girls do. We would spend hours and dozens of disposable cameras having someone take pictures of us while we posed in different outfits and in different locations. We had intentions of sending these pictures out to all of the modeling agencies, although I'm not sure we ever actually did. I still have many of these pictures in a scrapbook, and I look back and smile. I had no idea how powerful my imagination was or that seeing these pictures and believing I could do it would lead me to places I never expected.

My dad's business was no longer flourishing in our small town, which is what led us to Florida. I remember having mixed emotions and being sad that I was leaving all of my friends but also being very excited about a new adventure. I was able to make friends quickly, and before long, I found myself in front of the camera yet again.

One of the girls I hung out with knew a photographer, and we gathered a group of girls together for a "friendship photo shoot." I remember being one of a few girls taken aside by the photographer and told, "You should be a model and have your own website. You're great in front of the camera." I was flattered being told that I resembled a young Britney Spears. I thought to myself, "It's actually happening." And happen it did.

We planned another shoot, and this time it was at my house on the patio around the pool. I had to wear several outfits and actually borrowed some of my mom's more adult clothes. We took hundreds of pictures of me, starting out more innocent to eventually me looking noticeably uncomfortable in some of the clothes. I don't remember any alarms going off in my head, but as I look back at some of those pictures, I think maybe I knew something wasn't right. My parents were caught up in their own lives and addictions, and it didn't take much convincing from the photographer or me to get the papers signed. It was nothing too inappropriate because there was a line we could not cross. Next thing I knew, right before my 15th birthday I was an "online model" with my own website to prove it. I was so caught up in what was taking place on my side of the website that it never occurred to me what was happening on the other side. Why were hundreds and eventually thousands of men paying to be a member of my website? It didn't hit me until I was far too accustomed to the money, excitement, and pampering that came with it all. It became a huge part of my life for the next 10 years. It often defined in my mind who I was. I was the wild, outgoing, confident website girl who had far too much freedom and money.

"Webmasters" are what my photographers were called, and I found myself with a few different ones. Oddly enough, one man who would be my webmaster the longest ended up becoming like a father figure to me. One day he would lead me to what would absolutely alter my life for the better. It is hard for people and for even me to fully understand, but our relationship with one another was not what you might expect. There was always a line we never crossed. It was as if God had placed us in one another's life. During some very difficult times when I was moving with my family from house to house and times when we had nowhere to go while my parents battled their addiction, the money from that website and help from him was what kept me, and sometimes my family, afloat. He was an intelligent man who had a successful career prior to this endeavor, and on our trips, I learned so much from him. I didn't know that inside he was fighting an emotional struggle to find his purpose, and overcoming life's struggles.

Once I turned 18, I branched off and started doing some more professional modeling. It was the first time I crossed the line of taking off my top and even did some artistic nudity, as they called it. The pictures were often really beautiful, and I was good at navigating my limits and (what I thought was) respecting myself. I started another website and eventually left the other behind. This is where I began crossing lines. The webmasters were very different and open to much more, so I became more open as well. I was able to keep some limits, but the lines definitely became blurred. I put myself in some very dangerous situations. I experimented with drugs. I flew all over, usually not knowing who I was meeting at the airport that day. After a couple of years, I knew the money was not worth it, and I found myself with the old website and the old webmaster I had known. Even this didn't last long though—you see this was when the one thing that would change everything for me came into play in the most unexpected way.

In the car on my very last trip to California, I sat listening and learning from that webmaster yet again. This time the subject was much different: Jesus Christ and what having a relationship with him meant. You see in those couple years I had ventured off, he had found God and himself in the process. Now, in the most unexpected way, I was being led to God. And I eventually led my family to God. Before we left California he took me to the Christian bookstore and bought me three books that would change my life. The Bible, Joyce Meyer's *The Confident Woman*, and Paul Young's *The Shack*. Flying home and reading The Shack, I had no idea how much my life, my heart, and my views would change over the years and how that trip would be a catalyst in my life. I have learned that judging anyone or any situation is wrong because you never know what's really going on behind the scenes and what God might be doing.

It's interesting how life is always changing, always evolving. They say if you're not changing, you're not growing. Today I look back at the past six years of my life, and I am amazed by everything that has changed—and, luckily this time, I am also amazed by the personal growth I've experienced as well! I've traded in my less admirable traits, bad habits, and old hang-ups in exchange for a satisfying addiction to self-growth. I am so grateful for the improvements I've taken on, but I cannot take credit for them. You see, that trip to California and accepting a relationship with Jesus is when, without me even noticing, my life started dramatically changing. Before Christ lived in my heart, I could look back over other recent years of my life and see a flood of changes, but little that amounted to growth or even to what average people call improvement. I was stuck in a cycle and didn't know how to get myself out. Now I can look back and see all the positivity that has come my way!

Difficult times seem to be a normal part of my life and history. I am not complaining; I actually embrace this. As I write this now, I am facing one of the more difficult periods in my life. I find more peace in those difficult times now, though. I feel I have God alongside me working through difficulties with me. I still have my times where I am a complete mess, and I struggle with understanding them. However, now I can walk through problems with more grace. I know that these struggles are refining me and bringing me closer to my life's purpose. I understand that I can take these hard times and in turn help others through what I have learned in my experience. I now know that struggles are an opportunity to find strength.

I think my biggest struggle was figuring out who I was if I wasn't the website girl. I went from feeling like I couldn't get any more confident to realizing that my so-called confidence was a facade I put on to conceal all my insecurities. I hit a low point where I had no confidence, and I had no idea who I was or what I had to offer. Then piece by piece, God built me up again. I have real confidence now, the kind that doesn't need validation from others telling me I'm beautiful or unique. I now know I am beautiful and wonderfully made, and I have never felt more secure in that. I am not afraid to be bold in who I am rather than who the world tells me I should be. Romans 12:2 says, "Do not conform to the pattern of this world, but be transformed by the renewing of your mind." My mind has truly been renewed, and because of my past and now my change of mindset I am truly unique and God can use me to help others.

Honestly, I wouldn't recommend my path and my choices, I am truly lucky that I am still here and that much worse did not happen to me. I remember a time when someone would mention God and I would shy away quietly thinking to myself "what a Bible thumper." I wasn't sure if God truly existed or if he was some form of human-made comfort. Now I know without a doubt he exists. There are things that have happened to me that have no other explanation, and I cannot describe to you the peace I feel now, even in the midst of struggle.

Being transformed has not been easy, and I still have a long way to go. I have had to let go of a lot of things because they were not enabling me to grow. I have to accept my weaknesses and work on them daily.

One of my biggest blessings in life has been my children. I am currently pregnant with my first little girl. I am so excited, but I also know I have a big challenge ahead of me. Our society teaches women that being sexualized is normal and even desirable. I can speak from experience that it only brings hurt and confusion. I know God has called me to help empower women to respect themselves when the world is screaming the opposite.

I am not ashamed to be who I am, to be the woman I was created to be past, present, and future. I do have some regrets, but I wouldn't change anything because without experiencing those things for myself I wouldn't have the perspective I have today. I wouldn't be as grateful as I am that God has changed my heart and mind in many ways.

I believe life is all about improvement and finding your purpose and way to help this world be a better place. You're always changing, growing, and becoming your best self. There are some aspects of my past that are both a struggle and a gift. Helping run my own website for 10 years gave me an entrepreneur mindset, one that has led me to a home-based business. I tend to think outside of the box when it comes to making money. However, I often take the hard work people do day in and day out to financially provide for granted. I am not afraid to put myself out there and take chances because being outgoing is second nature to me, yet sometimes I am a bit too open and come on a little strong. I'm learning balance.

There is always a silver lining. There is always a way to turn that struggle into strength and soar.

I do struggle with the same feelings of inadequacy that I am sure everyone sometimes struggles with, and I find that if I simply put one foot in front of the other and keep moving forward one step at a time, God directs me. It is amazing the way things have unfolded before me in the most unexpected way. Being part of this book is one of those things.

I am determined to be the best kind of sexy I can be and to help other women do the same. That may seem confusing to you, so let me explain a bit. Sexy now means something completely different to me. Sexy is no longer what I look like, what I'm wearing, or based on how many people are showing me attention. Sexy is being confident in who you are and being humble, kind, and non-judgmental. Sexy is so much more than I can get into right now, so I will tell you about a blog I am in the beginning stages of called, of course, The Best Kind of Sexy. Sexy is not simply what the world is telling us it is; it is so much more than that!

I have big plans for The Best Kind of Sexy, including writing a book, talking on stages all across the world helping women, and much more. I will let

God direct my path and stay patient as I know I will continue to grow along the way and step into whatever he has for me at that point in my life. In the meantime, I will continue to embrace the lessons I have learned thus far, and I hope I can encourage you to do the same.

Always respect yourself and be bold in who you are, but not too bold. Work every day to better yourself and hold your head high no matter what the world is telling you.

Find your confidence in God, and if not in Him, then in a higher power than yourself. Please do not find your confidence here in this crazy world.

Remember, there is always a way to turn any struggle you are going through into a strength. There is a way to help others and move closer to your purpose.

 TWEETABLE
Sexy is no longer how many people are showing me attention. Sexy is being confident in who you are, being humble, kind, and non-judgmental.

 *Alicia Lowry is a Christian blogger and entrepreneur. Her home-based business through ACN helps families and businesses save money and gives individuals the opportunity to build a sustainable business to finance their dreams. To learn more about Alicia's passion, The Best Kind of Sexy, teaching the world to be confident, humble, kind, and non-judgemental, email*

thebestkindofsexy@gmail.com

CHAPTER 36

Failure Is the Surest Path To Success

by Adrian Shepherd

Skeptical? Read on. No one wants to fail, but everyone wants to succeed. The problem is that, as most successful people will tell you, in order to succeed, you're going to have to fail first.

Me, I didn't just fail once, but twice. Talk about lucky, right? Ironically, a failed partnership, losing a small fortune, and three men got me to where I am today. So how did they help me become Asia's number one time management and joint venture expert?

My first big failure was a partnership that went awry. We had all the right intentions, but the wrong plan. I'm not even sure we had a plan. Early on, I could see that we were in for a rocky ride unless some changes were made. I didn't have any mentors at the time, so I decided books were my best bet to find answers we needed.

What I learned led me to make some tough decisions that actually cost us a third of our customer base. Normally that would be akin to financial suicide, but I had done the calculations and we actually were able to increase revenue by a stunning 50%. Outsiders looked at our company and thought it was just a matter of time till we folded up shop. However, it was precisely those decisions that not only saved our company but also allowed it to prosper.

In the end though, I decided to part ways with my partner because we just didn't have the same vision. Rather than go through a long legal battle, I chose to leave a sizeable amount of money on the table. I felt my sanity was worth more than a few dollars.

It hurt my bank account and cost me a few sleepless nights, but this is where it all started.

I remember picking up Rich Dad Poor Dad. It opened my eyes to a whole different way of looking at business. But my "aha" moment came when I was listening to one of Tony Robbins' mentors, Jim Rohn, give a lecture. He said two things in particular that set me down my path of self-improvement.

The first was "Don't wish it were easier, wish you were better." It's something Jim Rohn is famous for saying, and when I heard it for the first time, it hit me like a sledgehammer. I have to admit; I hadn't thought about it that way. Many people complain about their work or company being too hard or stressful. Newsflash, it's not going to get easier. There will inevitably be challenges no matter where you work or how well you plan.

Jim Rohn taught me to go to work on myself and that, in doing so, I'd be better equipped to handle whatever comes my way. He was right. The stronger I became, the smaller problems got.

The second thing he said that really changed my outlook on life was "Set a goal to become a millionaire for what it will make of you to achieve it." I'd always thought that financial success was the goal, but Jim set me straight and made me realize that financial success is simply a reflection of who we are.

My second and more painful failure was entrusting a financial advisor with a quarter of a million dollars. Not only did he fail to grow it, but he also put it in four different investment vehicles that all went belly up. You've got to hand it to him—that takes skill. I'm not going to lie, seeing that money disappear was tough. But as Charles R. Swindoll said, "Life is 10% what happens to you and 90% of how you react to it." I made a decision that I wasn't going to let it beat me, and instead used it as fuel to make me better.

Two mistakes, one big lesson: be careful whom you trust. It's amazing how people, even with the best of intentions, can lead you to disaster if you're not careful.

Either of these occurrences could have ruined me. Certainly, there were rough times. I wanted to throw up when I learned that I had lost $100,000 overnight, and I'm not ashamed to admit that I shed a few tears along the way. But here's the thing, they were just events. Life will knock you down from time to time; the question is whether you're strong enough to get back up.

The life of an entrepreneur isn't always easy. I remember seeing a graph depicting just what an entrepreneur must go through to get where they want to go. Essentially, it started with excitement, then they took a few missteps which leads to anger, then more excitement, desperation and then finally, somehow they achieve success.

Jeff Bezos talks about failure in this way. "People love to focus on things that aren't working. That's fine, but it's incredibly hard to get people to take bold bets. And if you push people to take bold bets, there will be experiments... that don't work."

The one thing I learned from these mistakes is...failing sucks. It sucks in school and it sucks in life. The only difference is, in school it's just one test or assignment. In life, failing can mean losing everything that is truly important to you—your marriage, your family, the privileged life you worked so hard to achieve. The only good thing about reaching rock bottom is that the only way to go is up.

Entrepreneurs often strike out on their own because they want to make a difference in people's lives. They are the risk takers and, sadly, some don't make it and turn back to the corporate ladder seeking refuge, licking their wounds. I certainly had my fair share of wounds, but without them, I wouldn't be where I am today.

With each of my failures, I learned more. Each problem led to another book, audio lecture, or DVD training. Reading or listening to ideas from people like Jim Rohn, Tony Robbins, Brendon Burchard, Dan Kennedy, Jack Canfield, Kyle Wilson, Brian Tracy, Jim Stovall, and Zig Ziglar transformed me. I'm not the man I used to be. When I started this journey, I was just your average English teacher. Today, I'm Asia's premier time management expert and joint venture broker. Talk about a transformation.

My first book, iSucceed, written back in 2010, wasn't the best-seller I'd hoped it would be. However, in the process of writing it, I became a better writer. In 2016, I co-wrote the book, Profitable Joint Ventures with Sohail Khan which is available on my website, and in 2017 I went on to become a contributor for numerous online publications including Thrive Global, Addicted2Success, and CEOWorldMagazine.

Failure often comes down to a few bad decisions or mistakes. But it's not important how many times you get knocked down. It's how many times you get back up. Thomas Edison isn't remembered for failing 9,999 times, because that 10,000th time, made him a fortune.

If you're not willing to ask the girl of your dreams out for dinner, she'll never say yes. The same is true in business. You've got to risk something going after your dreams.

I may have lost a business and more than $250,000, but here I am, better than ever.

TWEETABLE

I was just your average English teacher. Today, I'm Asia's premier time management expert and joint venture broker. @isucceedbook.com

Adrian Shepherd started his career as an ESL teacher in Japan but today focuses on consulting with executives and companies on productivity and joint ventures. His background helped him develop The One-Bite Time Management System (TMS), a revolutionary new system based entirely around simplicity. Download his free report on the 5 big productivity traps at http://adrianshepherd. com. You'll find his articles on Inc.com, HuffPost, Thrive Global, Addicted2Success, Influencive, and CEOWorldMagazine.

Connect at www.linkedin.com/in/isucceedbook/.

He is based in Osaka, Japan.

CHAPTER 37
Change
by Nick R Bradley

One of the iconic images of Eastern philosophy is the lotus flower gloriously blooming from a pool of mud. Simply put, this is a poignant portrayal of the reality that in somber situations that are, at first, seemingly barren, bleak, and infertile...growth and progress is available to those who continue to sow the seeds of optimism and imagination.

This has always been a strength of mine, seeing the potential in a person rather than residing in their current situation.

As a mentor to some of the best golfers and now the best businessmen in the world, it has been my calling for 25 years to see beyond a client's current condition and provide them with the tools of authentic change and the wisdom of committing to the habit of growth.

I will submit to you that sometimes this is not easy. Sometimes, there is only mud to work with and no seed left within the person you are attempting to help. But rather like the potter who crafts a beautiful figurine from a lump of formless clay, it is your task to first see potential and secondly to have the pupil or client morph into that potential. Change is the culmination of work in the right direction.

Let's examine this process of permanent change a little deeper.

Phase I

It will be your experience that mobilizes the ability to see change in yourself and others.

Experience is the wisdom to look back and gather yet the capacity to similarly glance forward and visualize desires. I say, "glance forward" for good reason for it is in the now and in this moment that all things happened and all things will happen.

Those who perpetually live in the future are the dreamers and not doers. It's ok, in fact essential, that you do dream your best intentions, but do not hang around in that dreamland for too long. Constant wishful thinking is an exercise in fantasy and is wholly impractical if you want to move from A to B.

When in the visualizing stage, you must develop two lenses. The first lens is the wide-angle, big picture perspective. Whilst in this mode, imagine everything in its finalized form; the look, the taste, the touch, the atmosphere, and the sound. The goal here is assimilating the experience and not the inner workings. During this time you can find yourself walking around your desire, flying over your desire, using your desire, or being around the future you, the person you desire to become.

The wide-angle lens is the easy part of change. Frankly speaking, who doesn't want happiness, wealth, a beautiful living environment, and health? Most people have desired these tokens of life, yet few can pull them all together in one happy existence. This is where the smaller, more introspective lens must now be pulled out.

The small lens magnetizes everything together, and like the workings of a watch, it ensures that the sum of the parts will indeed create the whole. However, the small lens is the biggest obstacle to success, and here's why....

Thomas Edison said, "Opportunity is missed by most people because it is dressed in overalls and looks like work."

It looks like work because in using the small lens, you are truly examining the situation, object, or person you want to create or manifest. Equal to the size of your dream is the size of the workload.

In the spectrum of clients, I have mentored and instructed (and still do) billionaires, royalty, world-class sports people, and thought leaders. Each one of these achievers accrued success using a vehicle called hard and smart work. Very few, if any, blunder into success.

The small lens reveals the processes, the steps, and the time it will require to assemble the working pieces the big lens initially beckoned you in with.

But the question remains, dear reader: Do you have the desire, or even more pertinently, the discipline and determination to follow through with the vision of the small lens? Desire, discipline, and determination are the principles, the unwavering and unchanging principles that success seeks when natural adversities and challenges are encountered.

There is no victory, no sense of achievement if it is plain sailing to your outcome, simply because a certain amount of resistance is good for a person. Kites only rise when pointing into the wind.

The three D's mentioned, are the attitudinal attributes that are woven into the fabric of ALL successful people.

Jump frequently between your wide and small lens; it will help you and the others that surround you to maintain perspective.

Phase II

The second phase of change is trust. Let's be clear, trust is a feeling and feelings can insight doubt as equally as they can insight courage and fortitude. When I look to mentor a student, or when I level with myself knowing deep down that I must improve an area of my life, the question of trust always arises and thus the question of genuine feelings.

It's no good being in the middle ground with this. Emotion is probably the prime motivator in creating change. I have personally witnessed this time and time again in professional sport.

Prolific champions have risen from poverty and struggle. Former winners have experienced unforeseen resurgences when the emotion of losing a parent or a mentor occurs. Battle battered, mentally scared competitors cannot ever again muster the emotional drive that once obsessed them to compulsively win. Emotion IS the driver of focused action.

If trust is an emotion or a feeling, then it is without doubt a trait that must be nurtured and groomed rather than a trait that is instantly acquired. How are trust and feelings nurtured and layered to the point where you simply cross over the line from being a visionary to someone who executes focused action?

The answer is preparation and planning.

As strange as it may seem, there is a common thread between peak performance sport, business success, and the fear of flying. The common denominator that links all three is fear.

Fear, the fear of failure, or indeed the fear of success, has snuffed out more chances of achievement than any other malady. It's a debilitating curse mainly of the mind. Well, I'd like to reduce FEAR into this empowering acronym.

*F*ALSE
*E*VIDENCE
*A*PPEARING
*R*EAL

Fear is only empowered through a lack of preparation (knowledge) and planning (process).

People fear flying simply through irrational preconceptions about planes. If they took the time to understand aerodynamic design, the physics of airflow, or the efficiency of jet engines, their fears would dissipate.

Since fear influences trust so dramatically, and trust ultimately decides your feelings, it's important and ultimately essential that you extinguish fear through the preparation and planning stage.

Again, I reiterate, the small lens reveals the detail that provides the potential and the probability of change. Embrace what the small lens illuminates because, simply put, you'll be ahead of the game...most people will not.

Let me add one further piece of advice during this second phase: Do not think that you can wing it and retain important details in your mind and expect results.

As clever as we are as humans, we think in linear circumstance. That is to say, that like trains pulling into the station, we can only think one thought at a time. This neurological trait explains many *happenings* as a human, least of all our old friend *impatience*.

The devil is in the details; follow these guidelines to master Phase II of change:

- Create a hierarchy of influence. What are your real priorities? Like dominos, we want everything falling in its best sequence.

- Acknowledge that there are some areas where you may need professional help or mentoring. Gone are the days of trial and error; none of us have time in the 21st century to run around herding information butterflies.

- Be aware that you will feel impatience during this stage. Impatience arrives because the brain cannot fathom why, when you can already see the big picture completed in all its glory, you cannot attain and own it now. Impatience prevails because again, your thoughts arrive like packages at your door, one at a time. So, become mindful that your thoughts will likely back up like a chronic case of mental constipation, which induces impatience, and in more chronic cases, neurotic characteristics.

- If there is one purpose for using the small lens, it is to induce feeling. Whichever this feeling may be, security or insecurity, is solely dependent on what the lens has uncovered.

The more facts you attain, the more accurate and self-facing your feelings and opinions will be.

Phase III

There is a school of thought that, once Phase I and II, are complete, Phase III is as simple as falling off a log. Whilst there is no question that Phase I and II are there to increase your faith to act, there are mindsets you should adopt prior to full engagement.

- *Expectations*

Always expect the best, but be prepared for challenges. This mindset alone provides you with a strategic plan A and a plan B for expectations. Plan A is correctly strategized around everything the big lens and small lens predicted, and thus because of this, we'd naturally expect the plan to roll out just as we envisioned.

Plan B is your safety net. Plan B is expectant of unforeseen issues and ready to face them head on when they arise. As an example, all commercial airline pilots have a manual at the ready in the event that there is a mid-flight problem. They don't start off with a pessimistic outlook. Pilots obviously operate from a position of logic working for them and their passengers, but in the event of an issue, the quick solution guide book is used.

So, your expectations will work almost on the same trajectory as your preparation, the more you prepare, the more you're flexible for the good and the bad.

- *Conviction*

"Do or do not, there is no try." said Yoda in Star Wars, Episode V: The Empire Strikes Back

If you have indeed got this far down the road, seen all you can see, and prepared all you can prepare, then you may as well give change your all. I can tell you first hand that exceptional businessmen and businesswomen are deadly decision makers. Once the evidence is in, it's an all or nothing mindset that sets them apart from the pack.

If Calvin Coolidge was correct, "Nothing in the world can take the place of persistence. Talent will not; nothing is more common than unsuccessful men with talent. Genius will not; unrewarded genius is almost a proverb. Education will not; the world is full of educated derelicts."

As Coolidge quite rightly suggests, persistence is paramount to success, but persistence is only realized through conviction. Without conviction, the essential ability to acknowledge why you do something is lost.

- *Courage*

It would be incredibly egotistical to suggest that any act of change wouldn't involve courage. All I can say on this matter is that I'd like you to think about how you will feel if you don't follow through with your convictions, feelings, and dreams.

"Regret for the things we did can be tempered by time; it is regret for the things we did not do that is inconsolable."
– Sydney J. Harris

Read the above quote again and let it ring home. Opportunities come to pass, they do not pause.

Change is a natural phenomenon to human beings. Look at the advances in medicine, science, and innovation. Some change is forced upon us, other times we change of our free will.

I want to leave you this from Shakespeare. It speaks of change and opportunity.

"There is a tide in the affairs of men, which taken at the flood, leads on to fortune. Omitted, all the voyage of their life is bound in shallows and in miseries. On such a full sea are we now afloat. And we must take the current when it serves, or lose our ventures." – Shakespeare

Follow through with Phases I, II, and III. Change is life and life is for living.

TWEETABLE
Some change is forced upon us. Other times we change of our free will. But, change is life and life is for living.

Nick Bradley is one of the world's top golf coaches, working with the best players on the PGA & European Tour. The bestselling author of 7 Laws of the Golf Swing, Nick is a also an international speaker and corporate trainer. His mission is to provide content that can be used immediately by his audiences to elevate their performance. To learn more visit https:// www.nickbradleygolf.com/.

CHAPTER 38

Never Give Up
by Todd Stottlemyre

"Never, never, never give up."
– Winston Churchill

In times of difficulty we are given the opportunity to choose perseverance. Success is derived from continued progress through the lessons failure teaches.

My story is no different.

In 1989, I was in my second season as a Major League Baseball player with the Toronto Blue Jays. Our team was off to a slow start, and I was bouncing back and forth from the bullpen, being a relief pitcher, to the starting rotation. I wasn't getting much playing time due to the inconsistency in my performance. It was early May, and before going to the ballpark, I got the news our manager Jimmy Williams had just been fired and our hitting coach Cito Gaston had been hired to take over as manager for the remainder of the year. I felt bad for Jimmy, but I thought the change might mean more playing time for me.

I arrived early to the stadium that day, and in the dressing room, as I approached my locker, I was told our new manager wanted to see me in his office. Walking into the manager's office, I had the vision that I was going to get promoted from the bullpen into the starting rotation. Cito asked me to take a seat opposite of him at his desk. The pitching coach was sitting to his left. Excitement and anxiety were pumping through my body at the same time. As Cito spoke, my excitement turned to fury in a nanosecond. Yes, I was going into the starting rotation, but not for the Blue Jays. I was being demoted back to the minor leagues for the second consecutive year.

My childhood dream of following in my father's footsteps was being challenged. This dream started in the majestic Yankee Stadium where my brothers and I roamed the field as toddlers while my father, Mel Stottlemyre, was pursuing his dream. My father was a three-time 20 game winner and a five-time all-star as a starting pitcher with the New York Yankees in his career. He was a legend, and he played with legends such as Mickey Mantle, Roger Maris, Whitey Ford, Thurman Munson, Bobby Murcer, and Yogi Berra, who was his first manager. Growing up with my father and his teammates inspired me to dream, and that dream was to play Major League Baseball.

I stormed out of the manager's office. I was furious, frustrated, and disappointed to say the least. I quickly packed up my baseball gear and headed to pack up my apartment in Toronto. I loaded my car and prepared for the long drive to Syracuse, New York. Before driving through the night to where I would meet up with my new teammates, I sat down to call my most trusted mentor, my father, who was currently the pitching coach for the New York Mets.

Dad answered, and I immediately told him the Toronto Blue Jays had just sent me back to the minor leagues. Before he could say a word, I went on a verbal rampage pouring out my anger and frustration. I was playing victim. I was playing the blame game, and I'm sure I sounded like a spoiled baby to my father. When I finally took a breath, my father spoke.

He said, "Todd, I would love to have you as a starting pitcher on my staff here in New York."

I was like YESSSSSSSS!!!

Then my father followed with, "But not with the way you are pitching now." He continued to say that I hadn't even come close to pitching to my potential. He reminded me how good he thought I could be.

Dad's words were tough but true. I was not ready to hear that I needed to get better. I was busy playing victim and feeling sorry for myself. Let's face it. It's always easier to blame others and play victim versus taking full responsibility for our own outcomes.

After hanging up the phone, it was time to hit the road. It was getting late in the evening, and I had a long drive ahead of me. I drove through the night, and it was long and quiet. My mind was racing with uncertainty. A dream that started back in Yankee stadium when I had just learned to walk was now in jeopardy. I was told by the world through my entire childhood that I was not like my father. I was asked thousands of times what was I going to do if or when I didn't make it.

I was starting to wonder if the world was right. What was I going to do? Playing Major League Baseball was all I ever thought of. I had practiced tens of thousands of hours preparing for my dream, and now, for the first time in my life, doubt started to creep in. Actually, doubt was taking over my whole body. I found myself planning to go back to school to get an education and get on with my life.

But then I would recall the conversation with my father. He still believed in me even though my belief in myself was running on empty. Even if I made it back to the major leagues, was I good enough to stay and make a career out of it? My mind was a see-saw battle. My dream was on shaky ground.

Early in the morning, I pulled into McArthur Stadium, the home of the Triple-A Syracuse Chiefs. I parked my car near the clubhouse as I watched the sunrise. I was tired and emotionally worn out. I had questioned my dream over the last six hours driving from Toronto to Syracuse. I leaned my seat back, closed my eyes, and my mind took me back to my childhood of roaming the grounds of Yankee Stadium: the birthplace of my dream. It was so real back then. I had inherited my father's environment. His teammates were not just my heroes, they were our family friends. I thought again on the conversation with my father. He believed that I was so much better than how I was currently performing. It all came together for me. It was not time to throw in the towel. It was time to persevere. My mindset had just turned 180 degrees. I could once again tap into the vision of my childhood dream. Hell, I could even smell the hotdogs in the ballpark. I had just decided that I was going all in. I was going to pursue the potential that my dad believed I had. I was going to become the hardest worker on the team. If I was going to fail, I was going to fail in front of the world. But if I was going to succeed. I was going to succeed in front of the world.

With my renewed mindset, every day was an opportunity to get better. I dominated Triple-A hitters. I was a man on a mission. I was obsessed to live out my dream.

Thirty days later, I got the call back to the big leagues. Once again I packed my bags, but this time I was going where I belonged, Major League Baseball. As I pulled out of the stadium in Syracuse, New York I made a vow that I was never coming back to the minor leagues.

The Blue Jays inserted me into the starting rotation, and I never looked back. I started game two of the American League Championship Series that year. I had the honor of playing with some incredible teams in Toronto where we became world champions in 1992 and 1993. I went on to play 15 years in Major League Baseball on three world championship teams. I amassed tens of millions of dollars. I played with some of the greatest athletes in all of sports. Many of my teammates are now in The Hall of Fame.

WHAT IF I WOULD HAVE QUIT?

I was inches from calling my career on that lonely drive from Toronto to Syracuse. My dream faced its darkest hour. I was vulnerable, and I had lost belief for the first time in my life.

WHAT IF I WOULD HAVE QUIT?

Yes, I would have missed out on 15 years of living my dream and three world championships. Yes, I would have missed out on tens of millions of dollars. Yes, I would have missed out on playing with some of the most gifted athletes in the world who I now call family.

The most important thing I would have missed out on is the belief that DREAMS do come TRUE.

When my dream faced its darkest hour, I could not see around the corner. Most give up when they are the closest to success, and I almost did too. I had no idea when I was ready to walk away that I was 30 days from not only living out my childhood dream but also living out a baseball career that accomplished three world championships.

If you get to your darkest hour, just remember you are getting close. That's the time to persevere. EVERYTHING IS POSSIBLE FOR THOSE THAT NEVER QUIT!

TWEETABLE
Everything is possible for those that never quit.

Todd Stottlemyre is a global entrepreneur, speaker, high-performance business coach, and a former professional athlete who played Major League Baseball for 15 seasons with three world championship teams. Todd earned the prestigious Branch Rickey Award and the Lou Gehrig Award in the year 2000. In addition to authoring Relentless Success, he has spoken to audiences up to 20,000 people and is truly inspiring others to dream big, teaching hopefuls to create goals, and providing a strategic roadmap through his online performance academy. It is Todd's mission to inspire others to live a life without limits. Follow Todd at www.toddofficial.com.

GET CONNECTED

**To Learn More About the
Kyle Wilson Inner Circle Mastermind**
Go To KyleWilsonMastermind.com
or send an email to info@kylewilson.com
with *Inner Circle* in the Subject.

▼

For details on upcoming events
Go to KyleWilsonEvents.com

▼

**Receive Your Special Bonuses for Buying
The One Thing That Changed Everything
Book**
Send an Email to
gifts@LessonsFromOneThingBook.com

WHAT OTHERS ARE SAYING

"Kyle, Friendship is wealth and you make me a rich man. Thanks for being a friend and partner all these years. Love and Respect!"

— **Jim Rohn (1930-2009), America's Foremost Business Philsopher**

"Kyle is simply a marketing genius! Every marketing dilemma I have ever had, Kyle has given me the brilliant and elegant solution on the spot. His consulting has saved and earned me hundreds of thousands of dollars over the years."

— **Darren Hardy, Former Publisher** *SUCCESS* **magazine**

"I have worked closely with Kyle Wilson for 25 years. He is one of the best all-around marketers, promoters, business-builders and entrepreneurs in the business today. We have generated more than a million dollars together."

— **Brian Tracy, Author of** *The Psychology of Achievement*

"Kyle Wilson, single handedly changed the way I look at life! And the way I participate in my own! His wisdom, loyalty and commitment to seeing people soar is unmatched in the industry. He is a spring board, sounding board and ultimately, a launch pad for anyone committed to pursuing their deepest dreams and ultimate goals! He is the most authentic mentor, friend and business parter I've ever had."

— **Erika De La Cruz, TV & Media Host, Speaker, Trainer and Author of** *Passionistas*

"Kyle is one of my old and dear friends and one of the smartest marketing guys I have had the opportunity to work with. He is the scrappy marketing guy. What I mean by that is, there are lots of guys who will put out business plans and do all kinds of nonsense and swing for home runs. Kyle is the real deal and finds ways to create product, add value, help people, build community, he's unbelievable."

— **Eric Worre, Founder of Network Marketing Pro and International Best-Selling Author of** *Go Pro – 7 Steps to Becoming a Network Marketing Professional*

"If wanting to break into the speaker, author, marketing world, no one knows and does it better than my 10 year friend, Kyle Wilson. He is responsible for millions of people having access to the brilliant wisdom of Jim Rohn and so many other business thought leaders. He attracts the best people to his Inner Circle, something I'm proud to be a part of. I'm also excited to be working on a new book with Kyle, Lessons From Sports. *Honored by his friendship."*

— **Newy Scruggs, 7x Emmy-Winning Broadcaster**

"Kyle is a valued friend, a marketing superstar and one of the most knowledgeable people in the personal development industry."
— **Robin Sharma, Best-Selling Author of *The Monk Who Sold His Ferrari***

"Kyle Wilson is not only one of my most valued friends and mentors, he is a marketing genius and brilliant business man always providing the most honest and insightful solutions to any challenge. I am honored to have him as my book partner and life long counterpart."
— **Jeanette Ortega, Best-Selling Author of *The Little Black Book of Fitness* & Celebrity Fitness Trainer**

"Kyle is one of the wisest and most brilliant marketing consultants in the world. He is the man behind the great marketing of Jim Rohn and so many other personal development legends. He is not only someone I've enjoyed collaborating and working with for over two decades, but also a close and valued friend. I recommend Kyle without equivocation."
— **Mark Victor Hansen, Co-Creator of *Chicken Soup for the Soul***

"Kyle Wilson is the best marketer I know. In the 20 years I have known him, everything he touches and every idea he generates turns into money. If you're looking for a degree of fame and a higher degree of wealth, I recommend you connect with Kyle as fast as you can."
— **Jeffrey Gitomer, Author of *The Little Red Book of Selling***

"Over the last 25 years, we've done several things together. Kyle is the only guy who has always under-promised and over-delivered on anything we have done together."
— **Tom Ziglar, CEO of Ziglar, Inc.**

"Kyle Wilson's insight, marketing acumen and business knowledge are guru level. His consulting, friendship and brilliant solutions have changed the trajectory of my career and life. His strategies don't just elevate, they transform you and your brand. "
— **Olenka Cullinan, Speaker, Passionista, Founder of Rising Tycoons & #iStartFirst Bossbabe Bootcamps**

Made in United States
North Haven, CT
26 January 2023

31657385R00127